The Legacy of Financial Literacy

Guiding My Child to Financial Success

By Jyotinath Ganguly

INDIA • SINGAPORE • MALAYSIA

Notion Press

No.8, 3rd Cross Street
CIT Colony, Mylapore
Chennai, Tamil Nadu – 600004

First Published by Notion Press 2020
Copyright © Jyotinath Ganguly 2020
All Rights Reserved.

ISBN 978-1-63745-322-3

This book has been published with all efforts taken to make the material error-free after the consent of the author. However, the author and the publisher do not assume and hereby disclaim any liability to any party for any loss, damage, or disruption caused by errors or omissions, whether such errors or omissions result from negligence, accident, or any other cause.

While every effort has been made to avoid any mistake or omission, this publication is being sold on the condition and understanding that neither the author nor the publishers or printers would be liable in any manner to any person by reason of any mistake or omission in this publication or for any action taken or omitted to be taken or advice rendered or accepted on the basis of this work. For any defect in printing or binding the publishers will be liable only to replace the defective copy by another copy of this work then available.

Contents

Foreword		*5*
Introduction		*9*
1.	2020 – An Incredibly Cruel Year	13
2.	Needs, Wants, Savings	17
3.	Secure Life and Health – Build the Moat	25
4.	Plan for Contingencies – Build the Fortress	35
5.	Portfolio Construction	69
6.	Goal Based Asset Allocation	79
7.	Asset Reallocation	93
8.	Personal Income Tax Benefits	97
9.	Conclusion	101
Acknowledgements		*107*
About the Author		*109*
Appendix: Why Invest in Equities?		*111*

Foreword

Living in a fast-paced world often forces us into prioritising short-term goals without considering future implications. In January 2020, I was traveling, eating incredible food at world-class restaurants and completing my final year of college. A few months before I was set to graduate, the COVID-19 pandemic struck and all of our plans were suddenly thrust into confusion and uncertainty, creating chaos but also allowing us an unprecedented time to pause. To think. The world shut down overnight, the stock market tumbled and we entered a time of quarantine. We began living a new normal - our conversations being dictated by the strength of our internet connections, and our biggest adventures constituting "dangerous" trips to the local grocery store.

As the news worsened, we watched the world unsuccessfully attempt to "stop the spread", fighting an uphill battle against an invisible enemy wielding the superpower of nature. As the pandemic deepened, our health-care workers and scientists rallied, and so did the global economic markets led by the technology sector. Amidst widespread unemployment and worsening prospects for industries like tourism and entertainment, Big Tech pounced on a rare opportunity, experiencing years of user growth within a few months by providing us platforms to stay connected, as the in-person meetings and classes we had taken for granted in the past were no longer an option. Health-care and vaccine production-related companies also saw astounding growth amid unprecedented demand and expectation in their search for an antidote to our predicament.

The extremity of the global pandemic and the economic responses clearly displayed the ebbs and flows of the market - the highs catalysed by government stimulus packages, vaccine news and technology sector growth; the lows triggered by COVID-19 infections rising to all-time highs and political uncertainty - giving us a real life crash course in market dynamics.

The biggest lesson we learnt was to invest as early as possible in life, because the market waits for no one. As people's savings and retirement hung in the balance of a destabilized economy, it became apparent that a strong, balanced, growing and diverse portfolio with a long history can do a lot to ensure peace of mind for life.

I had a lot of help from my dad in figuring out how to successfully manage my portfolio - not only in the current economic atmosphere, but for the years to come. It took a lot of conversations, a lot of reading, and some time, but I'm so glad I started the process. In the past few months, I have been able to set up my future self and family for financial success and I am grateful to all of the resources I had at my disposal. My dad, my family, and I hope this book acts as a guide to help you through your journey of finding your own financial security and success. The best time to take the first step is today.

Adit Ganguly
St. Louis, MO, USA
November 2020

Introduction

1. How do I safeguard my child's education?
2. How do I save for our family vacation?
3. How do I provision funds for a health emergency?
4. How do I prepare for unplanned job loss?
5. How do I secure a financially comfortable retirement?

Questions such as the above are increasingly being asked across the world, particularly due to the impact of the COVID-19 pandemic.

This compilation is the outcome of my conversations with my child during the continuing (at the time of writing) COVID-19 (coronavirus) pandemic. This discussion is an effort to build a platform of awareness that would lead to financial freedom and success by means of effective planning to achieve life's goals.

Background

Financial literacy is recognized as a critical skill that is widely lacking among senior students and young earners across the world.

In India, 66% of household financial savings are kept as bank deposits and cash while only about 7% of non-insurance household savings are financial (Reserve Bank of India, June 2020).

According to HSBC's India report, The Future of Retirement, nearly 68% of the working age population expect their children to support them in their retirement, perhaps due to their unpreparedness. In reality, only 30% retirees are actually getting such support (Fortune India, May 2019).

In the USA, a report finds only 16% of millennials qualify as 'financially literate' (Yahoo Finance, Feb 2020).

Only 24% of millennials demonstrate basic financial literacy in the USA (National Endowment for Financial Education).

Disclaimer

The discussions with my child are introductory in nature, aimed at explaining concepts to a student embarking on a career and seeking an introduction to the world of personal financial planning, an understanding of the nature of individual and family goals and a working level understanding of investment options to build and preserve wealth.

The clarifications are not claimed in any way to be comprehensive. The content is based on my observations, research and experience as a parent, not as a professional financial planner. No part of this book should be construed as investment advice. I will not be responsible for any consequences that any reader may face as a result of the points discussed. Readers are urged to study and analyze their requirements based on individual financial, family and career situations.

Only financial assets have been addressed. Physical gold and real estate examples are not in scope, being largely unregulated in India, with significant amounts of unaccounted money being involved.

Chapter 1
2020 – An Incredibly Cruel Year

Parent to Child: Several words and phrases have been used to describe the year 2020. Crazy. Forgettable. Topsy turvy. Unprecedented. Uninstall the virus and reboot. A one year pause in the history of the world. The worst year in recent history.

Your final semester in-person classes were stopped in March 2020 and moved online. Your graduation happened online. Classes for your next program experienced a delayed start. Meanwhile, the world came to a screeching halt during Q1 2020. Businesses downed shutters. Jobs began to disappear. The pandemic began its global spread. Thousands of virus infected citizens died around the world. Q2 2020 was far worse. Q3 2020 showed mixed signals as the second COVID-19 wave appeared in many countries. We are now in Q4 2020 and economies are hesitating to restart.

Management gurus have opined that the world's businesses can be impacted by external, macroeconomic factors beyond the control of businesses, represented by the acronym PESTEL: Political, Economic, Social, Technological, Environmental and Legal.

Going back only about a hundred years, we realize that a number of Health emergencies have devastated the world, destroying lives and livelihood. The Spanish Flu (1918-20) killed more people than the World Wars, Vietnam War and Korean War combined. (Source: Brainerd, Elizabeth & Siegler, Mark V, 2003. "The Economic Effects of the 1918 Influenza Epidemic," CEPR Discussion Papers 3791, https://tinyurl.com/yyrqcrpz).

Several smaller outbreaks have happened since, including SARS in 2003 and H749 in 2013. (Source: Wuqi Qiu,1 Cordia Chu,2 Ayan Mao,3 and Jing Wu. "The Impacts on Health, Society, and Economy of SARS and H7N9 Outbreaks in China: A Case Comparison Study." https://tinyurl.com/y58coh9t).

The SARS-Cov-2 virus hit us with the COVID-19 disease in Q4 2019. Over a million people have died in less than a year, and irreparable losses have been faced by individuals, families, businesses, countries and the networked world. According to the BBC, India's GDP contracted about 24% during Q2 CY 2020. (Source: https://tinyurl.com/yxm5cu7s).

According to the World Health Organization (WHO), countries reported widespread disruption of many kinds of critical mental health services:

Over 60% reported disruptions to mental health services for vulnerable people, including children and adolescents

(72%), older adults (70%). Around three-quarters reported at least partial disruptions to school and workplace mental health services (78% and 75% respectively). (Source: https://tinyurl.com/yykounsa).

Researchers have yet been unable to establish the origin of the SARS-Cov-2 virus. While scores of vaccine development programs are ongoing, the world is awaiting confirmation on the efficacy and timelines of availability of vaccines.

Worse still, there is no telling when the next deadly virus might emerge out of a wet market, or from a misdirected bio-weapons program in a lab.

The availability of effective "preventives" and "curatives", both in the required volumes as well as with target effectiveness, and efficient distribution mechanisms are unknown as of now.

Exhibit 1: Macroeconomic Factors Impact Business

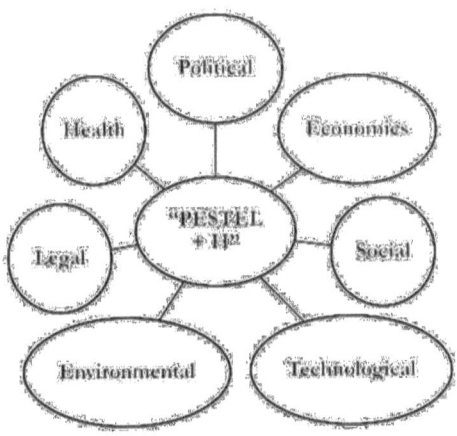

The need to secure one's financial future has emerged as a critical imperative during the months of lockdown that have been rolled out across the world. My suggestion is for management experts to add "H" indicating "Health emergencies" to the well accepted PESTEL macroeconomic parameters (Exhibit 1).

Meanwhile, youngsters like you need to get on with building your financial fortress and a deep, defensive moat around your lives.

You've got to tell your money what to do or it will leave.

– Dave Ramsey

Chapter 2
Needs, Wants, Savings

Question: Please help me understand the financial planning journey you undertook over the years, your primary considerations and lessons learnt.

Answer: Having graduated from college and about to enter the workforce with a zero financial base, my first step was to provision for life insurance and health insurance. The second step, which happened over the next several years, was to start learning the art of saving and investing. The process of learning, re-learning, implementing and correcting has been an extremely long journey spanning several decades. Every market crash has brought up a fresh perspective and lessons: 2000, 2008 and 2020, not forgetting the several mini crashes in between. Unfortunately, market peaks and crashes have a habit of showing up every now and then, which we need to mentally prepare for, and take corrective action, to the best of our abilities.

Planning for Needs, Wants, Savings

Based on my experience, it would be extremely useful for individuals and families to classify expenses according to categories and also over timelines in years. The outcome would be an effective understanding of key expenses and the tentative roadmap. Performed collectively, the planning experience has the potential of benefitting all members of the family over their life cycles.

The critical prerequisite is that individuals need to develop a mindset that facilitates judicious saving and investing. Capital market returns are at best uncertain and even appear to be following a downward trend over the years. My suggestion is that youngsters begin to assess the following two approaches.

Approach 1: "Save first, then spend" which is a conservative approach, versus Approach 2: "Spend first, then save" which may be termed a rather carefree approach. It is indeed a useful differentiation that youngsters need to clearly understand.

Keep in mind (1) "build the moat" expense category that I referred to (mandatory insurance – against external attack), followed by (2) "build the fortress" category (build and preserve wealth – equivalent to improving resources and supplies).

Expenses ideally need to be conceptualized to occur over phases of life, with the identified expenses comprising "must have" (needs) and "good to have" (wants). Finally, the critical element that needs to be planned for is the retirement corpus which may turn out to be the "resources and supplies" for several decades after active work and income stops (Exhibit 2).

Do not save what is left after spending, but spend what is left after saving.

– Warren Buffet

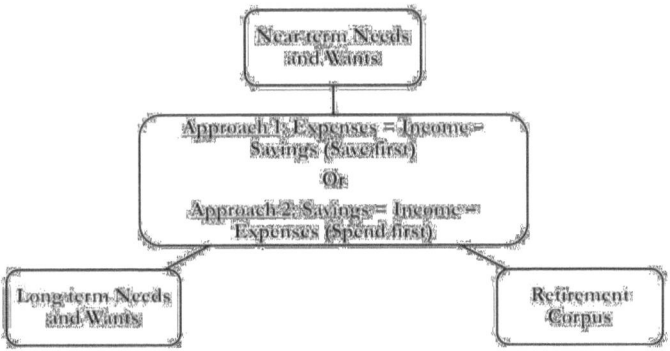

Exhibit 2: 'Save First' Approach Is Recommended

Diving deeper, a look at the spends reveals many sub-categories (Exhibit 3).

Exhibit 3: Types of Expenses

Life insurance	In the event of loss of life, nominee receives contracted benefits	Mandatory
Health insurance	Annual consulting, Diagnostics, Hospitalization, Pre- and post-hospitalization	Mandatory
General insurance (non-life)	Vehicle, home, accident, business travel, leisure travel, adventure travel	Some mandatory, some optional
Life basics	Home, food, clothing, education, transportation, vacation, jewellery, wedding	Needs
Lifestyle, discretionary	Expensive vacation, expensive home, expensive clothes, expensive car, expensive jewellery, flashy wedding, gambling	Wants
Inflation	Varies across countries, unpredictable, indirect expense	Almost invisible!

Life and health insurance is considered mandatory (except for those that can afford a life without either). Accident insurance is recommended. The 'needs' category of expenses are those that constitute the basic necessities such as food, shelter and education. The next category is that comprising the frills or 'wants'. Finally, one must not ignore inflation which continues to eat away into savings, including savings for retirement.

Question: This seems to be an interesting approach, with an emphasis on savings. Based on your experience, would you be able to provide a guideline regarding how people like me would need to divide expenses and savings?

Answer: In addition to understanding the approach of dividing needs and wants, it would really help to periodically revisit the expenses under needs and wants since these categories keep changing over time, driven by necessities on one hand and temptations on the other. The fundamental mindset shift that is needed is to make a commitment to save a proportion of your income. Typically, the range of 20% to 30% is considered a useful guideline (Exhibit 4).

Exhibit 4: Planning for Needs, Savings, Wants

Examples of self and family goals (includes needs, wants, loan instalment repayments)

Short term (Up to 5 years): Education (self), Emergency, Home, Insurance, Lifestyle, Marriage (self), Vacation, Vehicle

Medium term (5 to 15 years): Education (child), Home, Lifestyle

Long term (over 15 years): Education (child), Home, Lifestyle, Marriage (child)

Retirement: Corpus for age beyond 60 years, Lifestyle

Provisioning for Needs, Wants, Savings

Question: Appears like we have an approach in place, which I may want to refer to as "strategy". How would you suggest I go about the "execution"? I suspect that would be harder?

Answer: I agree with your observation, it is the execution capability that makes or breaks any strategy –

> from humble to grand – that is put together by the management of any business.

Keeping in view that execution needs to be consistent over a lifetime consisting of several decades, the following thoughts would help, several of which are unpredictable and may even appear to be unfavourable.

1. **Market returns vary**, impacted by Macroeconomics (global), Microeconomics (local), returns from investment instruments with different characteristics (equity, debt, commodities, real estate).

2. Market returns are **impossible to predict**.

3. Some expenses are **mandatory**, such as Insurance premium payments.

4. Core **needs** are hard to postpone or cancel, such as food, shelter, clothing, education, transportation and maybe a basic wedding.

5. **Wants**, however, may be postponed or cancelled, such as expensive jewellery, expensive cars and expensive vacations.

6. **Inflation** quietly eats into the value of savings, almost invisible, this is a major factor that needs to be considered.

7. Regular income may **stop unexpectedly**, a result of being declared redundant at work, or resignation from work, or the business experiencing a slowdown

8. In view of the above, it is strongly recommended to build a corpus for **emergency expenses**, after mandatory insurance has been paid for. For youngsters and young earners, building the emergency corpus may take several years, but it has to be done, with focus and patience.

9. **How much** should you invest? The amount varies from person to person. The answer is **any amount**: start with Rs 1,000 per month or any amount, as early as possible.

10. The next step is to plan for **long term portfolio growth** and **retirement corpus**.

The approach indicated above, in a nutshell, is the recommended approach to provision for needs, wants and savings.

Money is only a tool. It will take you wherever you wish, but it will not replace you as the driver.

– Ayn Rand

Chapter 3

Secure Life and Health – Build the Moat

Secure your Life

Question: You indicated that insurance is the first step in the financial planning journey. What was your experience like, and at what stage in your life?

Answer: Looking back, I now realize that my first step towards financial security was rather uninformed and inadequate. My first job had just happened after my Master's program. My well-meaning Dad called his "Insurance agent" friend Mr. P. and asked him to help me with life cover. Mr. P. showed up and magnanimously sold me an 'Endowment Policy' with a 35-year premium payment duration. I was covered for Rs 1,50,000 (Rs. 1.5 lakhs) which was a princely sum 30 years ago. To put it in perspective, the coverage amount may not even pay for a year or two of school fees today.

Mr. P. explained with a twinkle in his eye that I would receive an amount of money greater than the sum assured after 35 years, my reward for paying the premium throughout the tenure, referred to as Bonus. The years went by, and I faithfully kept paying the annual premium year after year. The scary part is that I realized quite late during my financial planning journey that had I popped off to the next world anytime during the past three decades, you and mom would have been left high and dry with Rs 1,50,000 plus a bit more of the accumulated Bonus. No way enough to pay for both of your livelihoods and your education.

Unfortunately, such Endowment policies continue to be mis-sold by commission greedy agents that promise payment of certain returns in addition to life cover. These statements tug on subscribers' heart strings. After all, what could be better than securing life and seemingly make a bit of money when the policy matures?

Several financial advisors I met over the years neglected to understand the holistic view of my financial security, and plans, if any. Consequently, they failed to highlight the risk that I was facing as a result of having bought a low coverage Endowment policy. Most financial advisors sold me random mutual funds. Some advisors even attempted to sell me further policies of this nature. Lesson learnt!

Remember that insurance agents earn fat commissions, a significant proportion of the first year premium, as a result of which getting you to sign up is their objective. Whether you continue to pay future premium is of no consequence to them, since future payments are not part of their annual appraisal process.

Think about it. Would any financially savvy Insurance service provider be a genius, capable of making you rich and provide life cover and remain profitable, all at the same time? Does such magic happen in the world? There has to be a catch! Not hard to figure out that insurance policies that promise monetary rewards typically yield in effect about 4% return to the subscriber. The 'returns' storyline needs to be dumped in the bin. Sadly, once you sign up, you will be charged massive 'surrender costs' should you wish to opt out. You are as good as hand cuffed!

The reality is that insurance service providers exist because of business reasons, not charity. The primary responsibilities of insurance service providers are towards their shareholders and balance sheet, more specifically, the profit and loss statement. Similarly, banks exist in order to be profitable and make their shareholders wealthy. A bank that sells insurance policies does so for business purposes.

The solution for folks like you is to choose a simple insurance policy without any returns attached, pay the least premium amount and make the difference work for you, maximized effectively in your own way, under your control.

In summary, my Dad and I got misled over 30 years ago. Fortunately, I have lived to tell the tale. Do take care, and don't get waylaid in similar fashion. Learn from my mistake! You are also highly likely to get seemingly attractive 'Money Back' policy offers such as "Pay 'W' premium for 'X' years, get 'Y' money back for 'Z' years". Ignore such offers!

Should any suave, smooth-talking insurance agent or bank representative or advisor come along offering you an Endowment plan or Money back plan or Return of premium plan (essentially life coverage and returns), my suggestion would be to firmly respond with:

1. Don't call me, I'll call you.

2. Call me next year.

3. "Naale Baa".

Question: Hmmm, that's valuable insight, Dad, about life insurance pitfalls to be vary of. What on earth is the "Naale Baa" message you are referring to?

Answer: Well, "Naale Baa" is the story of a ghost that was rumoured to haunt neighbourhoods in Bangalore, India during the 1990s, before you were born. The intentions of the ghost were never clarified. However, residents devised an innovative scheme to confuse the ghost. They put up signs along streets and outside their homes. The signs said: "Naale Baa", which in the local Kannada language translates to "Come tomorrow". Clever, was it not? The idea was to send the ghost into an infinite loop. The message would be "Come tomorrow" every day, for ever and ever.

Getting back to financial planning, any advisor that does not display empathy towards your financial security probably deserves similar gentle guidance.

Now that we have figured out that "cover plus returns" policies must never be considered, how much "pure life cover" should you plan for? The simplest Insurance plan available is known as Term Insurance. Pure cover, affordable, low premium, no frills, no feel-good returns, no promises of bonus pay out. Just what you need.

Factors to be considered while buying life cover:

1. Number of dependents or expected dependents (including parents).

2. Loans, and expected payment period.

3. Life insurance policies begun at a younger age tend to be easier to get approved, with lower premium payments.

4. Older individuals would need to pay higher premiums, or may find it hard to get insured because of diseases that may creep in later in life, increasing risk.

5. Insurance cover needs to cover outstanding debts and interest, and all expected liabilities including basic needs and a few selected wants.

6. A cover of Rs 1 crore (Rs 10 million) and upwards is recommended (subjective).

7. Death benefit needs to be adequate to replace income, increased cost of living and additional expenses expected over the remaining work life.

Takeaway (life insurance)

1. Always buy **Term life insurance**, for Rs 1 crore or Rs 10 million or higher.

2. Keep it **simple**.

3. **NEVER** buy returns oriented policies.

4. Buy **online** to avoid paying commission to agents.

5. Document the policy, claim **process** and contacts.

6. Invest the money you have '**saved**' by not buying policies that offer returns.

7. Remember **"Naale Baa"**.

8. **NEVER mix Insurance and Investment.**

Term life insurance is a good defensive game plan.

– Dave Ramsey

Secure your Health

Question: Thank you for the quick lesson on choosing life insurance. My take away is that I need to opt for Term insurance policies. Now, can you please help me understand tips and tricks around health insurance?

Answer: If you thought life insurance is complex, wait till you begin to understand health insurance!

Happy to state that my self-assessment report card on health insurance has turned out to be in the green. My corporate employers have, over the years, provided health cover for mom, you, me and my parents. However, about 20 years ago, I opted for personal health insurance (in addition to the cover provided by my employer at that time). I was keen to maintain the two policies in parallel, because my objective was that the personal insurance cover would kick in and cover loss of employer insurance due to situations such as loss of job, resignation and ultimately retirement.

Below are the main points to keep in mind and seek answers to, from the prospective health insurance provider:

1. Coverage amount per person.

2. Maximum claims per year per subscriber.

3. Increase in coverage due to annual "no-claim bonus".

4. Coverage of existing diseases and conditions.

5. Critical disease cover.

6. Period of no coverage after signing up.

7. Diseases and conditions that will never be covered.

8. Eligible diagnostic centers.

9. Eligible hospitals.

10. Pre-hospitalization coverage.

11. Post-hospitalization coverage.

12. Sub-limits for hospital rooms, nursing, doctors, consumables, diagnostics and so on.

13. Co-pay clause which refers to the amount that the insured must pay in the event of a claim.

14. Whether the insured must pay and claim reimbursement or whether the 'Cashless' coverage is supported, at least in selected hospitals.

15. Documentation of the policy and claim process for your family members to understand.

It is recommended to sign up for health insurance early in life. The flip side is that health insurance policies that have been signed up decades ago might end up providing inadequate coverage as the years go by, due to the constant increase in the cost of healthcare products and services.

Therefore, consider the following options (and others with similar coverage) to augment initial health insurance that you sign up for:

1. Top-up options

2. Family floater options

3. Critical disease options.

Takeaway (health insurance)

1. Plan for **continued health insurance** coverage, during and after formal employment.

2. **Lack** of health insurance may result from loss of job, resignation and retirement.

3. It may be possible to **port** your employer's group Insurance coverage to private pay for personal coverage after resignation or loss of job or retirement.

4. Consider personal health cover in **parallel** to your employer's group coverage to ensure continuity in case of complications such as sudden loss of job and consequent panic, leaving you with little or no time to remember to implement health insurance portability.

5. Check the **fine print** that may number in the hundreds.

6. Reconfirm annual **no-claim bonus** additions and exclusions.

7. **Reconfirm** claim processes and document clearly so that all family members are aware of the process and contacts.

8. Consider **add-on options** to enhance coverage to required levels as time goes by.

Think of an economy where people could be an artist or a photographer or a writer without worrying about keeping their day job in order to have health insurance.

– Nancy Pelosi

Chapter 4

Plan for Contingencies – Build the Fortress

Investment Options

Question: Having attempted to read about investment options, I am actually rather confused by the number of options available to build wealth. I need help to understand options and considerations that would help me choose optimally.

Answer: I do agree, the options are indeed several, and would be confusing to beginners. You have probably heard of wealth building and wealth preservation options as well as industry terms, which I would like to clarify.

Investment options:

1. Bank deposits, mutual funds, stocks and bonds are referred to as **conventional investments**.

2. Financial assets such as private equity, venture capital and commodities and physical assets such as real

estate, jewelery, art, antiques and wine are examples of **alternative investments**.

An important concept is that a mix of the at least two asset classes is recommended to construct a long term investment portfolio, for reasons that will be explained shortly. However, for quick understanding, using a multi-asset financial portfolio would be equivalent to not putting 'all eggs in one basket'.

Looking below the surface, a number of sub-investment options are available (Exhibit 5).

Exhibit 5: Investment Options (Financial, Physical)

Bank, Post-Office deposits	Widely recognized, easily understood, high-comfort level, returns known ahead of time.
Debt or Fixed Income or Bonds	Loan money to businesses or governments and expect to earn interest while capital is expected to be preserved.
Direct Equity (Stocks)	Buy stocks, become part owner of a business, rewards include capital growth and dividends.
Indirect Equity (Mutual Funds)	The Asset Management Company (AMC) pools investors' money and invests in stocks, rewards all investors.
Commodities (Gold, Silver, Copper, Platinum, etc)	Invest in financial assets and profit from global price increase; Physical refers to assets such as Gold jewelery.
Real Estate	Invest in stocks of Real Estate businesses (financial); Physical refers to commercial and residential properties.
As per Government policy	Certain financial investments enable you to leverage policy based exemptions to reduce taxable income and income tax.

Terminology

Being a potential investor beginning your journey, I suggest you bookmark several terms that are commonly encountered during the process of assessing and planning investment options (Exhibit 6).

Exhibit 6: Frequently Used Terms

Alpha	Measures the performance versus a benchmark index, positive alpha indicates outperformance versus the benchmark, baseline being 0.
Beta	Measure of volatility compared to the market, more than one indicates greater volatility than the market, baseline being 1.
Capital appreciation	Growth in the base or invested amount.
Correlation	Relationship between performance of assets such as Equities, Bonds, Commodities: -1 (inverse) to 1 (in step).
Diversification	Leveraging multiple investment options, equivalent of 'not keeping all eggs in one basket', objective is to reduce risk.
Risk	Possibility of capital erosion or reduction in rate of interest.
Volatility	Variations or spikes in the value of asset or interest, over time.

I have not forgotten your question regarding the choices to build wealth over time. Conceptually, there are two basic approaches to increase wealth:

1. Grow the base amount or principal or capital, referred to as **capital appreciation**.

2. Get rewarded or even increase the quantum of your reward over time. This is referred to as **interest** for 'debt investing' and **dividend** pay-out for 'equity investing'.

Unfamiliar terms? I will try to explain the two popular approaches of debt and equity investing in the next two sections.

How many millionaires do you know who have become wealthy by investing in savings accounts? I rest my case.

– Robert G. Allen

Debt Investing Basics

The most widely known debt investment option is to deposit your money with a bank, and earn a pre-determined rate of interest. The interest earned from savings banks has dropped significantly over the years. Therefore, bank deposits are recommended only to hold your money that would be needed for expenses over the next few months, and not for serious investments.

Moreover, I am not going to discuss Indian Government backed deposit options such as:

1. Pradhan Mantri Vaya Vandana Yojana (PMVVY)
2. Senior Citizen's Savings Scheme (SCSS)
3. Post Office Savings Schemes.

The above deposits are considered safe, and are typically leveraged by conservative individuals at retirement stage. Returns are not spectacular. Moreover, lock in periods may apply and taxation implications need to be factored in.by investors.

Several market linked debt investment options are available, though the percentage of the population taking advantage of such options is rather limited, according to data from the Reserve Bank of India.

A brief introductory description might read like this: debt investing deals with loaning your money and getting rewarded through interest payment. Perhaps you recall the concepts of simple interest and compound interest that you had learnt in school?

Regarding market linked debt investing options, whom could you loan your money to, safely? The answer is: to reputed businesses and governments.

Asset Management Companies (AMCs) make it easy for investors like you and me by pooling investors' funds and loaning out the money to businesses and governments on our behalf. AMCs sign a 'contract' or 'paper', referred to as a 'bond'. The duration of the bond may vary from Overnight to Ultra Short Term (months) to Short Term and Medium Term (years) to Long Term (may be decades). Investors receive the principal amount back at the end of the tenure of loan, as per the terms of the contract.

So, imagine you have loaned out money – to a business or government – would you feel relaxed and have nothing to worry about? Is that possible in life? Perhaps, in a few cases.

Realistically, is there a likelihood of losing the capital that you have loaned out? What if the business goes belly up? Even reputed brands have been known to go out of business. What if the government goes bust? Well, that's probably unlikely, at least with the governments that you and I are likely to deal with. Government is considered to be the safe investment option that I alluded to earlier. From the terminology perspective, the lack of safety of your loaned amount is known as **Credit risk** in the world of debt investing.

Secondly, what if you need your principal amount back, for whatever reason, and wish to opt out of the contract? Would your principal be available to you should you need it during the period of the sign up tenure, at the moment you need it? If so, Liquidity is said to be high. In case there is a possibility of the business or government not being able to return your money, the bond is said to have **Liquidity risk**. Reasons for Liquidity risk include mass redemption requests from investors, which may happen to not so well reputed funds during market panic situations.

Further, long duration bonds present a different kind of risk. The risk is that the accepted interest rate may change during the course of the bond tenure, either upwards or downwards, due to availability of fresh bonds offering different interest rates compared to your sign up rate. Availability of new bonds might result in changes in the demand for the bonds that you hold. The reason is that due to new interest rate offered by new bonds, the older bonds of the type that you hold would experience increased demand if the new bonds offer lower interest rates, or would experience reduced demand if the new bonds offer higher rates. This possible interest rate fluctuation is known as **Interest rate risk**. Another possible reason is that the bonds may be perceived to carry some kind of risk, as a result of which demand may reduce, resulting in lowered price.

To understand debt investing risks, on a lighter note, consider the following scenario. How safe and liquid would an investor's money likely to be when loaned to a student like you, just starting out on the journey of life, with no income and prior proven financial history? On the other hand, how safe would an investor's money likely to be when loaned to someone like me, earning an income and debt free? No offence meant, but that's a quick take on two risks associated with debt investing: Credit risk and Liquidity risk.

With the above simple introduction to risks in debt investing, let me now describe three possible options of loaning out your money. Try not to forget, in the midst of all the technical buzz words, that your primary objective is to preserve wealth and earn some interest.

Consider the following scenario where you have three options available to loan out your money to:

1. A well-established business
2. A shaky business
3. Government.

Below is a summary of the three debt investment opportunities, with the different risks indicated (Exhibit 7).

Exhibit 7: Debt Investment Options

Debt Investment Options	Option 1	Option 2	Option 3
Loan your money to	Profitable business	Unstable business	Government
Terms of loan	1 year duration, 6% rate of interest	5 years duration, 7% rate of interest	Fully secured, 10 years duration, 5% rate of interest
Safety of Principal	High, proven	Lowest	Highest
Liquidity Risk	Low	Highest	None
Credit Risk	Low	Highest	None
Initial Interest Rate	Medium	High	Low
Interest Rate Variation Risk	Low	High	Highest

In summary, the safety consideration is paramount to ensure the availability of the money that you have loaned out and expect to earn a reward from. Equally important, you expect the principal amount to be returned to you at some point in time, either at the end of the tenure or earlier, should you need the base amount back.

The easy to remember acronym to assess the feasibility of Debt mutual funds is "SLR" – Safety, Liquidity, Returns.

"SLR" is the order of priority recommended for investors to consider while choosing debt mutual funds for investment (Exhibit 8).

From the safety perspective, the only debt bonds that are considered safe are Government backed papers, known as G-Sec or Gilt or Sovereign "SOV". The disclaimer is that investors trust the Government not to collapse. The disadvantage associated with "SOV" papers is that durations are often very long, such as 10 years, 20 years, and so on, during which time the interest rates may vary significantly depending on the demand for those bonds, resulting in high volatility that is often observed. Therefore, the risk associated with Government bonds tends to be Interest rate risk, and not Credit risk or Liquidity risk.

Private enterprises seek to borrow investors' funds to grow their business. In such cases, investors often compromise safety to varying degrees. Conservative investors prefer a profitable business with an impeccable financial history, a lower bond duration, and lower interest rate risk.

Exhibit 8: Debt Investment Priorities

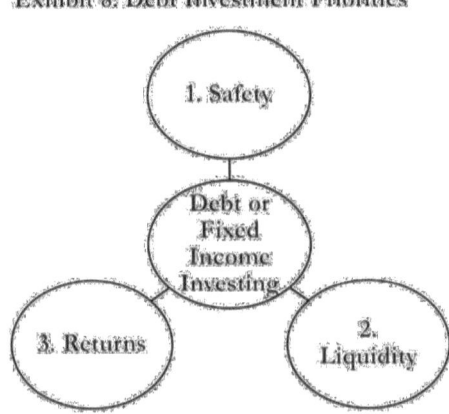

The next safety level after Government bonds that investors commonly look for is "AAA", held by government backed businesses and corporates of good standing. The AAA rated bonds are generally considered to be "almost" as safe as government backed bonds.

Adventurous investors sometimes seek businesses that may not be in a healthy shape, but offer higher rates of interest in return for the risk taken. This class of bonds are known as **Credit Risk** bonds. Yes, such options do exist for risk tolerant investors!

Now, a word about bond ratings, which are a standard indicator in the world of debt investing. Globally reputed ratings agencies such as S&P and Moody's are authorized to certify the quality of bonds offered by governments and businesses. Their scope of work is to assess governments and businesses in terms of financial parameters, and issue ratings certificates that indicate the likely safety of investors' funds. Rating levels certified are SOV, AAA, AA and so on.

A partial summary of non-Government bond ratings is indicated below (Exhibit 9).

Exhibit 9: Bond Grades and Risk Rating

Moody's	Standard & Poor's	Grade	Risk
Aaa	AAA	Investment	Lowest
Aa	AA	Investment	Law
A	A	Investment	Low
Baa	BBB	Investment	Medium
Bb, B	BB, B	Junk	High
Caa, Ca, C	CCC, CC, C	Junk	Highest
C	D	Junk	In Default

Source: Investopedia, Oct 2020

Question: This is rather interesting, quite a revelation. I would need some time to digest the inputs. In order to help me along to determine my initial investment needs, would you be able to put together a ready-reckoner of sorts?

Answer: Your request is indeed a great idea. For your quick understanding, indicated below is a summary of recommended debt investing options to maximize safety and liquidity, minimize credit risk and interest rate variations (for the near term) and to build a rock solid corpus (for retirement). So, what lies in between? The volatile and fun option known as equity investing.

Recommended fixed income investment roadmap may be categorized as follows (Exhibit 10):

1. Debt: Duration 2 to 2 years (with bank deposits)
2. Debt: Retirement corpus.

Exhibit 10: Commonly Used Debt Investment Options

Investment Duration	Debt Instrument	Interest Rate Risk	Credit Risk	Liquidity Risk
2 to 3 years	Short Term Debt Funds	Low	Low if largely AAA	Rare if largely AAA
Retirement*	PPF, NPS, EPF, VPF	Defined periodically	None	None

*Indian Government backed safe instruments preferred for Retirement corpus
- PPF (Public Provident Fund: full tax free withdrawal possible, no annuity compulsion, cannot be attached by creditors)
- NPS (National Pension Scheme: equity and debt options, complex taxation, withdrawal partially tax free, partially compulsory for taxable annuity)
- EPF and VPF (Employee Provident Fund and Voluntary Provident Fund: employer maintained, tax free transfer to employee on retirement)

Takeaway (debt or fixed income investing)

1. **Funds for immediate use and emergency use:** Bank accounts with auto sweep facility.

2. **Funds for two to three years:** Well rated corporate debt mutual funds with contracted duration of 2 years, known as Short Term mutual funds, offering safety and relatively lower interest rate volatility risk.

3. **Funds for retirement corpus (may be decades away):** Government-backed debt assets, being safe and non-volatile in nature (Public Provident Fund, PPF; National Pension Scheme, NPS), leveraging the Power of Compounding.

4. **Funds for salaried employee's retirement corpus:** The mandatory Employee Provident Fund, EPF, as well

as the highly recommended, optional Voluntary Provident Fund, VPF.

5. Further, the PPF (Public Provident Fund) asset has the advantage that it **cannot be attached by creditors**, even if you go bankrupt at any time.

Question: I realize that I have learnt an interesting approach to maximize availability of funds for ongoing, near term expenses. However, I see that there is a significant gap between the 2 year bucket and the retirement objective. What kind of investing option should I consider for the many decades stretching towards retirement?

Answer: For the rather long period between the next few years and retirement, the optimal approach would be to choose primarily equity investment assets, described in the next section. Long term equity investments are strongly recommended to overcome the impact of inflation and to build wealth.

Risk comes from not knowing what you are doing

– Warren Buffet

Equity Investing Basics

For equity investing, the two most common routes are the long established Direct stock buying and Indirect (relatively recent, now recommended as the first step). Other mechanisms such as Derivatives, Futures, and Options are beyond the scope of this discussion.

Equity Investing – Direct

Question: I recall you mentioning that my Granddad used to invest in stocks many years ago, and that is how you picked up the basics. I seem to have gathered that stock picking is a complex and specialized process – an art and science – demanding considerable skills and attention from the investor. Is my observation correct?

Answer: Several decades ago, before internet and digitization of financial assets happened, stock investing used to be done by learning from daily newspapers and the annual (extremely fat!) Bombay Stock Exchange handbook. The Indian National Stock Exchange (NSE) did not exist at that time. There was no TV either, with the benefit of 'no noise', but the flip side was there was no real time data available. Interestingly enough, many good businesses of the past either do not exist or have merged or have been acquired, while many of today's top businesses were not born at that time, obvious reasons being new technologies, new services, new businesses and new business models. Therefore, the debate on buy and hold strategy is subjective, depending on investment objectives and type of portfolio.

How easy or hard is it to pick sticks? Well, business success depends on several factors. Revisiting management concepts of customers and ecosystem (cannot help but do that!), the scenario may be described using the exceedingly famous Porter's Five Forces model that I have taught budding management graduates.

Dr Michael Porter had stated that business success depends on key factors spanning:

1. Customer preferences
2. Competition
3. Bargaining power of suppliers
4. New competitive entrants
5. Product or service substitutes.

Industry forces, business capabilities, customer relevance, supply chain and distribution strengths as well as market presence play an important role in business success, in my opinion, beyond analysis of ratios such as PE (Price to Earnings ratio). Therefore, I critically analyze external market and sales parameters while picking stocks directly, using Dr Porter's framework as a guideline (Exhibit 11).

Exhibit 11: Porter's Five Forces

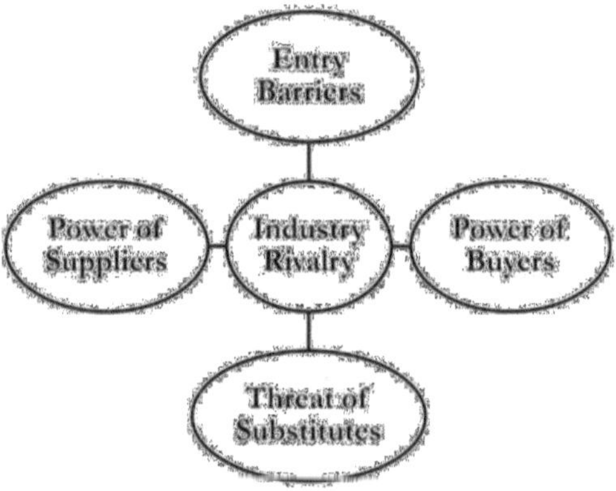

- Entry Barriers
- Power of Suppliers
- Industry Rivalry
- Power of Buyers
- Threat of Substitutes

Source: Dr Porter, Harvard Business Review, 1979

Specifically, I attempt to deep dive and study parameters such as the market that the business is in, market growth, market positioning, market dominance, business model, value chain and resource analysis, go to market capabilities as well as select financial trends and ratios that help me shortlist stocks that I may want to consider adding to my portfolio.

Do remember that every consideration would not apply for every stock, particularly for emerging segments or emerging businesses. Some analytical filters would not apply to established businesses that are in the midst of diversifying (Exhibit 12).

A strong dose of discretion is advised, along with careful analysis of management profile, as well as governance track record.

Exhibit 12: Stock Picking Needs Some Study!

Consistent 'Sales' and 'Return On Capital Employed' (ROCE) Growth
⬇
Reinvest profits to Grow business; Pay dividend; Transfer to reserves
⬇
High barrier to entry; Dominance in segment or in emerging segment
⬇
High Reserves to Equity ratio; Low Debt to Equity ratio
⬇
'Shortlist stocks for direct equity investment; Diversify across segments'

One more point. While my investment timeframe is long term, I do a small quantum of tactical investing or fun investing, such as sectoral and emerging trends investing. Adds to the thrills and spills due to the ups and downs of the stock market. Taking informed risks is often a great deal of fun!

Takeaway (direct equity investing)

1. As an equity investor, you are considered part **owner** of the business.

2. Your participation level is consequently higher than fixed income investing, earning **rewards** such as capital appreciation and dividends.

3. **Risk** levels are higher, and the impact may be high in case you have not chosen stocks wisely.

4. Choosing stocks is not necessarily difficult with the right approach, however the challenge would be to stay **focused** on your basket of stocks and not get distracted by **unqualified advice** received from diverse sources.

Go for a business that any idiot can run – because sooner or later, any idiot probably is going to run it.

– Peter Lynch

Equity Investing – Indirect

Question: I need to understand the rationale behind indirect equity investing and the logic used to choose investment options. How would you suggest I go about choosing mutual funds?

Answer: The choice in the equity mutual fund landscape is rather broad, with several twists and turns, and needs some understanding of terms such as market capitalization of businesses.

First, the process. At a high level, investors pay Asset Management Companies (AMCs) that pool in investors' capital and choose stocks on their behalf. The stocks may be from the Large Cap, Mid Cap or Small Cap segments or a combination such as Multi Cap.

Market capitalization is an extremely commonly used term, often referred to as market cap. It measures the market value of the publicly traded company's outstanding or unrestricted shares. Market cap indicates the company's net worth or stock valuation. Stocks are also picked with reference to industry segments such as Banking, Healthcare and Information Technology, depending on the mandate of the mutual fund.

The advantage of indirect equity or mutual fund investing is that designated Fund Managers manage the stocks in the portfolio. Periodic purchase and sales of stocks by Fund Managers does not impact investors' personal taxation (Exhibit 13).

Exhibit 13: Investing in Stocks vs Mutual Funds

Direct Equity (Stocks)	• Investor assesses and chooses stocks • Investor buys the stocks on the Stock Exchange • Investor benefits from Capital appreciation and Dividend pay-out as an individual • Investor deals with tax implications • Investor responsible for risk and reward
Indirect Equity (Mutual Funds)	• You pay an Asset Management Company (AMC) • The designated Fund Manager pools money from investors and picks stocks (in the case of Actively Managed Funds) • Quality of stocks determine performance of the fund • Capital appreciation and Dividend pay-out to investors is a pool • Investor does not pay tax due to Fund portfolio churn • Index Funds and Exchange Traded Funds (ETF) growing in popularity, both are low cost options that track respective Indices

The investor's risk tolerance, market knowledge, and time to study the market are key factors that influence the choice between the direct and indirect methods of investing in equities. Direct equity investing (stocks) is suitable for experienced investors who have the time and skills. Young investors and those with limited time and skills (and interest!) are advised to go through the route of equity mutual funds in order to diversify, lower risks and build a safety net.

The downside is, however, the fairly hefty Asset Management fees that investors need to pay to the AMC. More on this aspect later.

It's not how much money you make, but how much money you keep, how hard it works for you, and how many generations you keep it for.

– Robert Kiyosaki

Benefits of buying the Mutual Fund Direct Plan

Question: I have heard about Dividend Option and Growth Option, and, Regular Plan and Direct Plan. Can you explain this, please, and the benefits and drawbacks?

Answer: Mutual funds offer two options to gain from profits: **Dividend Option** and **Growth Option**. In the Dividend option, profits (dividends from shares) are paid out to the investor, but you need to check for tax implications as per country tax policies. In the Growth option, profits are reinvested back, and there are no tax implications until you redeem the units.

Regarding **Direct Plan** and **Regular Plan**, which is a controversial topic of sorts: from the evolution perspective, investors had to, for several decades, invest in mutual funds through an intermediary known as a Distributor or Advisor. This intermediary would earn a commission for helping me buy, this was how I went about mutual fund buying when I started. In 2014, the Direct Plan was launched and investors could buy directly from the AMC without the need for an intermediary, as a result of which the investor has benefitted by way of lower management fees.

Over the past few years, however, zero fee based intermediaries have developed a business model with the AMC whereby these new age intermediaries advise investors and hold their portfolio, yet offer Direct Plans with zero commission.

The difference between the Direct Plan and Regular Plan is that the Regular Plan has a higher expense ratio that is deducted from investors' returns. Returns of Direct Plans have the potential of galloping significantly from the long term perspective, as indicated in the Exhibit below. Most investors appear to be blissfully unaware of the financial disadvantage of buying the Regular Plan.

The difference in returns to investors tends to be around 1% in favour of investors that buy the Direct Plans (Exhibit 14). This difference compounds over time.

Exhibit 14: Mutual Funds: Benefits of Direct Plan vs Regular

	Regular Plan	Direct Plan
Monthly SIP amount (Rupees)	25,000	25,000
Investment Tenure	30 years	30 years
Annualized Return	12%	12%
Expense Ratio	2%	1%
Final Corpus (Rupees, after SIP tenure)	51,700,000	64,600,000
Outperformance by Direct Plan (Rupees)	12,900,000 (over 24%)	

Source: https://www.paisabazaar.com/mutual-funds/direct-vs-regular-mutual-funds/

Direct vs Regular Plan		Direct	Regular	Difference
	Investment (Rupees)	10,500,000	10,500,000	0
	Investment tenure	5 years	5 years	0
Mutual Fund 1	Average 5 year return	20.34%	19.24%	1.10%
	Final return (Rupees)	25,23,271	24,10,315	1,13,256
Mutual Fund 2	Avg. 5 Year Return	19.69%	18.63%	1.06%
	Final return amount	24,56,345	23,49,485	1,06,860
Mutual Fund 3	Avg. 5 Year Return	31.39%	30.92%	1.07%
	Final return amount	40,05,946	38,46,183	1,59,763

Source: https://groww.in/blog/direct-vs-regular-mutual-funds-examples

The drawback of choosing the Direct Plan without **adequate knowledge** is that investors may end up making incorrect choices, due to:

1. **Recency bias**, which is the temptation to consider recent or the past few Quarters performance data, and not develop a holistic approach. Factors to consider would ideally include long term performance, drawdowns or volatility, changes in fund mandate, fund manager history, performance when the market was dropping, performance when the market was going up, performance during a market crash, and so on.

2. **Concentration risk**, which is investing in a non-diversified portfolio such as only equity or only debt or investing in more than one mutual fund from the same market capitalization segment or industry sector or any investment that leads to significant stock overlap underlying the mutual funds.

3. **Advise from diverse sources**, which may include uninformed friends and family, discussions on TV that are not aligned with your plan, as well as content from random web sites.

Takeaway (mutual fund investing)

1. Conduct your own **research**.
2. Take **informed decisions** instead of ad-hoc decisions based on random advice

3. Assess your **personal financial roadmap**.
4. Assess your volatility **risk tolerance** (fund performance varying over the years).
5. Buy mutual funds under **Direct Plan** instead of Regular Plan to avoid paying commission to AMCs.
6. Be careful of agents trying to mis-sell you **Regular Plan** mutual funds to meet their sales targets.
7. **Dividend Option** may result in tax to be paid, please check country specific policies.
8. Should you choose the **Growth Option** you have to account for the redeemed value as income for that financial year.

Know what you own, and know why you own it.

– Peter Lynch

Active Mutual Fund Performance Unpredictability

The primary reason for investing is to build wealth. However, tracking the performance of mutual funds across market capitalization segments over time may result in a bout of dizziness.

Representative data from the Indian mutual fund industry indicates the constantly changing ranking of mutual funds over the years. The reason is that each mutual fund contains a portfolio of stocks, so the varying performance characteristics of the underlying stocks that comprise the mutual fund determine the overall performance of the fund. Therefore, the fund manager needs to track a number of stocks. The averages number of stocks held by mutual funds appears to be about 50 (fifty).

The returns of mutual funds are measured against a standard metric known as the return of the **Index** for the segment, developed for various market capitalization segments such as Large Cap and Mid Cap and combinations, as well as industry sectors such as Banking.

To reinforce understanding, a comparison of mutual fund performance has been shown for four categories of mutual funds: Large Cap, Mid Cap, Small Cap and Multi Cap, the latter consists of stocks from across segments in proportions that comply with the regulator's guidelines. The data indicates the highly fluid nature of the ranking positions occupied by mutual funds from several AMCs. The mutual funds ranked by performance are seen to be constantly on the move as data from several time periods is examined.

Representative ranking data of mutual funds across the four market capitalization segments indicated above, over a span of 3 years, 5 years and 10 years has been tabulated. The data is as of November 4, 2020.

Large cap mutual fund data: Below is a glimpse of the performance of mutual funds from the Large Cap segment. Notice that the performance and ranking of top funds keep changing, like a game of musical chairs (Exhibit 15).

Exhibit 15: Large Cap Mutual Fund Performance (3Y, 5Y, 10Y)

Large Cap	3 years
Axis Bluechip Fund - Growth Large Cap Fund	9.12%
Canara Robeco Bluechip Equity Fund - Regular Plan - Growth Large Cap Fund	8.25%
Edelweiss Large Cap Fund - Growth Large Cap Fund	5.89%
BNP Paribas Large Cap Fund - Growth Large Cap Fund	4.61%
L&T Mastershare Unit Scheme - Growth Large Cap Fund	3.42%
Large Cap	**5 years**
Axis Bluechip Fund - Growth Large Cap Fund	11%
Canara Robeco Bluechip Equity Fund - Regular Plan - Growth Large Cap Fund	10%
Mirae Asset Large Cap Fund - Regular - Growth Large Cap Fund	10%
HSBC Large Cap Equity Fund - Growth Large Cap Fund	7%
IDFC Large Cap - Regular Plan - Growth Large Cap Fund	7%
Large Cap	**10 years**
Mirae Asset Large Cap Fund - Regular - Growth Large Cap Fund	12%
Canara Robeco Bluechip Equity Fund - Regular Plan - Growth Large Cap Fund	10%
Axis Bluechip Fund - Growth Large Cap Fund	10%
BNP Paribas Large Cap Fund - Growth Large Cap Fund	10%
SBI Blue Chip Fund - Growth Large Cap Fund	9%

Source: Moneycontrol.com, Nov 4, 2020

So, which Large Cap mutual fund would you consider, to deliver the returns that would be suitable for your roadmap?

Which AMC or mutual fund would you go with? Performance versus the Index is not widely available.

Mid cap mutual fund data: Now take a look at the performance of mutual funds from the Mid Cap segment. Again, notice the performance numbers and rankings change, another game of musical chairs (Exhibit 16).

Exhibit 16: Mid Cap Mutual Fund Performance (3Y, 5Y, 10Y)

Mid Cap	3 years
Axis Midcap Fund - Growth Mid Cap Fund	10%
Quant Mid Cap Fund - Growth Mid Cap Fund	5%
PGIM India Midcap Opportunities Fund - Growth Mid Cap Fund	5%
Invesco India Mid Cap Fund - Growth Mid Cap Fund	4%
DSP Midcap Fund - Regular Plan - Growth Mid Cap Fund	3%
Mid Cap	**5 years**
DSP Midcap Fund - Regular Plan - Growth Mid Cap Fund	11%
Kotak Emerging Equity - Growth Mid Cap Fund	10%
L&T Midcap Fund - Growth Mid Cap Fund	9%
Invesco India Mid Cap Fund - Growth Mid Cap Fund	9%
Taurus Discovery (Midcap) Fund - Growth Mid Cap Fund	9%
Mid Cap	**10 years**
Invesco India Mid Cap Fund - Growth Mid Cap Fund	15%
Edelweiss Mid Cap Fund - Regular Plan - Growth Mid Cap Fund	14%
HDFC Mid-Cap Opportunities Fund - Growth Mid Cap Fund	13%
BNP Paribas Mid Cap Fund - Growth Mid Cap Fund	12%
L&T Mid Cap Fund - Growth Mid Cap Fund	12%

Source: Moneycontrol.com, Nov 4, 2020

So, which Mid Cap mutual fund would you consider, to deliver the returns that would be suitable for your roadmap?

Which AMC or mutual fund would you go with? Performance versus the Index is not widely available.

Small cap mutual fund data: Thirdly, below is a look at the performance and ranking of mutual funds from the Small Cap segment is shown. A significant game of musical chairs, once again (Exhibit 17).

Exhibit 17: Small Cap Mutual Fund Performance (3Y, 5Y, 10Y)

Small Cap	3 years
Axis Small Cap Fund - Growth Small Cap Fund	7%
Quant Small Cap - Growth Small Cap Fund	6%
Quant Small Cap - Growth Small Cap Fund	6%
Kotak Small Cap Fund - Growth Small Cap Fund	2%
Union Small Cap Fund - Regular Plan - Growth Small Cap Fund	2%
Small Cap	**5 years**
Axis Small Cap Fund - Growth Small Cap Fund	11%
Kotak Small Cap Fund - Growth Small Cap Fund	9%
Nippon India Small Cap Fund - Growth Small Cap Fund	9%
L&T Emerging Businesses Fund - Regular Plan - Growth Small Cap Fund	8%
DSP Small Cap Fund - Regular Plan - Growth Small Cap Fund	7%
Small Cap	**10 years**
Nippon India Small Cap Fund - Growth Small Cap Fund	15%
DSP Small Cap Fund - Regular Plan - Growth Small Cap Fund	14%
Franklin India Smaller Companies Fund - Growth Small Cap Fund	11%
Kotak Small Cap Fund - Growth Small Cap Fund	11%
Quant Small Cap - Growth Small Cap Fund	9%

Source: Moneycontrol.com; Nov 4, 2020

So, which Small Cap mutual fund would you consider, to deliver the returns that would be suitable for your roadmap?

Which AMC or mutual fund would you go with? Performance versus the Index is not widely available.

Multi cap mutual fund data: Finally, a look at the performance and ranking of mutual funds from the Multi Cap segment. Once again, like the above cases, absolutely no predictability is observed.

So, which Multi Cap mutual fund would you consider, to deliver the returns that would be suitable for your roadmap (Exhibit 18)?

Exhibit 18: Multi Cap Mutual Fund Performance (3Y, 5Y, 10Y)

Multi Cap	3 years
Parag Parikh Long Term Equity Fund - Growth Multi Cap Fund	11%
Quant Active Fund - Growth Multi Cap Fund	10%
UTI Equity Fund - Growth Multi Cap Fund	9%
Canara Robeco Equity Diversified - Regular Plan - Growth Multi Cap Fund	7%
PGIM India Diversified Equity Fund - Growth Multi Cap Fund	6%

Multi Cap	5 years
Quant Active Fund - Growth Multi Cap Fund	13%
Parag Parikh Long Term Equity Fund - Growth Multi Cap Fund	12%
UTI Equity Fund - Growth Multi Cap Fund	10%
DSP 3 Years Close Ended Equity Fund - Regular Plan - Growth Multi Cap Fund	10%
Canara Robeco Equity Diversified - Regular Plan - Growth Multi Cap Fund	10%

Multi Cap	10 years
Invesco India Multicap Fund - Growth Multi Cap Fund	12%
UTI Equity Fund - Growth Multi Cap Fund	11%
Kotak Standard Multicap Fund - Growth Multi Cap Fund	10%
Quant Active Fund - Growth Multi Cap Fund	10%
Canara Robeco Equity Diversified - Regular Plan - Growth Multi Cap Fund	10%

Source: Moneycontrol.com, Nov 4, 2020

Which AMC or mutual fund would you go with? Performance versus the Index is not widely available.

The outcome, as you can well observe, is a continuous shift in delivered performance by any given mutual fund, over the years.

And guess what! Investors like you and I continue to pay Asset Management Company fees to the extent of 1% to 2% for the typical equity mutual fund.

Unpredictable performance, variable performance, often low performance compared to the Index and the need to pay high fund management fees are some of the reasons for the increase in the popularity of another type of mutual funds called **Index funds** that deliver performance according to the baseline performance rating for market capitalization segments or industry segments. The fees paid for Active fund management tend to be significantly higher than the fees paid for Index fund management.

Therefore, the concept of Index investing is increasingly being considered in India at this time, while Index investing has become quite mature and well established in several other economies.

Highly revealing data from Indian markets indicates the underperformance of Actively managed mutual funds compared to respective Indices over a 5-year period ending Dec 31, 2019.

A staggering number of funds: **27% to 97%** of actively managed funds, have **underperformed** the index across equity and debt funds. The performance data of Actively managed versus Index mutual funds is published by SPIVA (S&P Dow Jones Indices Versus Active), a division of S&P Global (Exhibit 19).

Exhibit 19: Active Mutual Fund Underperformance

Percentage of funds that underperformed the benchmark.
Data as of Dec 31, 2019

Fund category	Comparison index	5 Yr %	3 Yr %	1 Yr %
Indian Equity Large Cap	S&P BSE 100	82.29	84.38	40.00
Indian ELSS	S&P BSE 200	78.38	88.37	70.73
Indian Equity Mid/Small Cap	S&P BSE 400 MidSmallCap Index	40.91	37.21	27.91
Indian Government Bond	S&P BSE India Government Bond Index	84.91	83.33	57.69
Indian Composite Bond	S&P BSE India Bond Index	97.78	78.26	82.76

Source: SPIVA indices, Oct 2020

To provide a view from another economy, there is significant data available from the US markets about the underperformance of Actively managed mutual funds.

According to the SPIVA U.S. Mid-Year 2020 Scorecard, most active fund managers in the U.S. underperformed the market over the past year. Among actively managed domestic equity funds, 67% lagged the S&P Composite 1500® during the 12 months ending June 30, 2020, and the majority of active managers underperformed their benchmarks in 11 out of the 18 categories of domestic equity funds.

(Source: Berlinda Liu, Director, Global Research & Design, S&P Dow Jones Indices, https://www.indexologyblog.com/)

Below is more data from the Indian mutual fund industry:

Mutual fund performance is ranked in four quartiles, with 25% of funds in each quartile. As per S&P Dow Jones Indexology research, only a tiny percentage of funds stayed in the first quartile of all rolling periods across six years (July 1, 2013 to July 30, 2019):

Large cap = 6.66%

Mid cap = 7.14%

Small cap = 9.09%

Multi cap = 3.84%

ELSS = 3.12%.

(Source: Livemint.com, Nov 20, 2020).

The question is: would you be lucky enough to identify those few funds that stay in the top 25% of the performance quartile year after year? Before investing, without the benefit of hindsight?

Probably not!

Consider the long term perspective. Young earners such as yourselves have an investment roadmap that could stretch several decades, such as 50 years or 60 years or 70 years. The compulsion to consider Index funds is highly valid. Besides, over time, Indexing constructs and choices would only improve in India, whereas the level of maturity has already been demonstrated in other markets.

Takeaway (active vs index mutual funds)

1. Conduct your own **research**, build your personal **roadmap**, assess your portfolio performance or **returns** requirement (value over time), assess your **risk** tolerance (**"4R"**).

2. If you invest in actively managed mutual funds, it is likely that you would experience **uncertainty and underperformance** compared to the Index.

3. You may be tempted to invest in the **latest high-performance funds** now and then **(recency bias)**.

4. If you keep adding mutual funds to your portfolio, you will end up helplessly watching your portfolio get **cluttered and hard to manage** over time, and get stressed out as a result.

5. Meanwhile, you continue to pay **high fund management fees** with vast **long term compounding losses**.

6. Do you have an investment **roadmap over 10 years?**

7. Is your investment roadmap likely to extend to **20 or 30 or 40 or 50 or 60 or 70 years?**

8. Are you considering leaving a **legacy** of financial assets for your future generation?

9. If so, consider **Index mutual funds** instead of actively managed mutual funds.

10. Be wary of agents trying to **mis-sell** you mutual funds based on their sales targets.

11. Carefully choose reference **websites and blogs**.

Question: The data is rather revealing. Can you please help me understand the approach you would recommend for diversified asset investing, particularly for me, in the early stages of my career, with a long investment horizon of several decades?

Answer: Given your long horizon, the preferred approach would be to invest across diversified assets with varying performance correlation. Recommended to consider a mix of Stocks, Index funds, Exchange Traded Funds. You may want to consider **one** actively managed hybrid equity fund, depending on the geography, maturity of index construction and active fund performance characteristics.

As briefly alluded to earlier, mutual fund investing has evolved into Index funds and Exchange Traded Funds, being low cost investment options where the assets track respective indices, without the need to rely on fund managers, without the need to pay high expense fees and without the need to experience unpredictably variable performance over time.

Moreover, the loss to the investor due to long term compounding and due to the payment of fund management fees can grow to be highly significant, as indicated above. A combination of direct plans (if needed) and Index funds would work in favour of long term investors.

Homework

You may want to try this Internet search using your favourite search engine: "How many Large Cap (or Mid Cap or Small Cap) funds have beaten the Benchmark Index over the past 30 years or 20 years or 10 years or 5 years in India (or USA)?"

Mutual Fund Risk-O-Meter (India)

Securities and Exchange Board of India (SEBI), based on the recommendation of the Indian Mutual Fund Advisory Committee (MFAC), reviewed guidelines for product labeling of mutual funds and the following scale has been decided. The Risk indicators are quantified to indicate risk in ascending order (Exhibit 20).

Exhibit 20: Mutual Fund Risk Level Summary

Risk Value	RISK LEVEL AS PER RISK-O-METER
≤ 1	Low
>1 to ≤ 2	Low to Moderate
>2 to ≤ 3	Moderate
>3 to ≤ 4	Moderately High
>4 to ≤ 5	High
>5	Very High

Source: SEBI, Oct 2020 https://tinyurl.com/y4r3ubsy

A summary of risks across debt mutual fund categories is lower (1 = lowest) while the summary of risks across non-debt mutual fund categories indicates higher risk (7 = highest).

Further, thinking back on the risks of debt investing, the three major risks are Safety, Liquidity and Returns. These factors are considered to produce the final rating indications, ranging from SOV (Government backed, G-Sec) to AAA (highest rated non-Government bonds), to AA, and so on, in descending order of rating quality.

Gold bonds are rated at 4, a neutral value, while equity oriented mutual funds are classified into ratings 5, 6 and 7, as indicated in the table below. Mutual funds containing real estate stocks are rated at the highest risk level (Exhibit 21).

Exhibit 21: Mutual Fund Risk Level Snapshot

Debt Mutual Funds	Risk Level
G-Sec, AAA credit rating	1
AA+ credit rating	2
AA credit rating	3
Etc.	
Macaulay duration <0.5 years	1
Macaulay duration >0.5 to <1	2
Macaulay duration >1 <2	3
Etc.	
G-Sec, AAA, PSU liquidity risk	1
Other AAA liquidity risk	2
AA+ liquidity risk	3
Etc.	

Equity, Gold, Real Estate Mutual Funds	Risk Level
Equity Large cap	5
Equity Mid cap	6
Equity Small cap	7
Equity Daily Volatility <1%	5
Equity Daily Volatility >1%	6
Gold	4
Real Estate	7
Etc.	

Source: SEBI, Oct 2020 https://www.sebi.gov.in/sebi_data/

Takeaway (mutual fund risk):

1. The Securities and Exchange Board of India has defined mutual fund **risk ratings:** 1 (low risk) to 7 (high risk).

2. **Debt** mutual funds are rated towards the bottom end of the scale (lower risk)

3. **Gold** mutual funds are rated at 4.

4. **Equity** mutual funds risk levels start at 5, with Large Cap funds.

5. **Mid Cap** and **Small Cap** mutual funds are rated at higher risk.

6. **Real estate** mutual funds are rated at the highest risk value.

To make the most of your money, I recommend sticking with mutual funds that don't charge a commission when you buy or sell.

– Suze Orman

Chapter 5
Portfolio Construction

Question: Picking up a thread from before, you mentioned the term "diversification". Can you please explain the relevance of this investment approach?

Answer: A core concept to understand is that investors face the Reward vs Risk dilemma. There is no such thing as a free lunch. Face it, you will not get rewarded unless you are prepared to take risks. Risks include possibility of loss in capital as well as reductions in interest rates or dividend returns. The well accepted fact is that risk aversion will probably lead to a depleted portfolio and inadequate support for the phase of life when income is likely to stop for most people. Therefore, the time to take informed risks is when investors are young. They have the benefit of time to recover from the sharp ups and downs that happen every now and then, and also to take a call regarding reducing risk gradually over the years. The mechanism to reduce risk will be explained in the following pages.

So, here are a few ground realities. Given that using one type of investment is equivalent to putting all eggs into one basket, it is strongly recommended to use a mix of investment types so that the overall basket results in a semblance of stability and reduced volatility.

To drive home the point, here are two analogies

1. Vehicle manufacturers offer a number of choices spanning factors such as vehicle form factor, engine capacity, boot capacity, automatic transmission and colour, among others.

2. Mobile phone manufacturers offer models with varying processor type, memory capacity, storage capacity, colour, camera features, and so on.

The reason for offering a diverse set of products is that due to varying customer preferences, a broader basket has a higher likelihood of appealing to a larger spectrum of customers. The number of customers addressed is increased. Further, should one or two model not sell, there is a possibility that some other models may sell well. As a result, the risk due to product concentration is reduced.

This approach resulting in a broad portfolio with each product behaving differently is known as diversification. From the asset class perspective, different asset classes such as equities, debt, gold, and others tend to display varying characteristics in terms of metrics that are used to define investment performance over time, as well as risk-related parameters.

Commonly used asset performance criteria include:

1. Capital appreciation
2. Safety
3. Rate of interest
4. Dividend pay out
5. Liquidity
6. Volatility.

The above terms would be familiar to you by now. This is a good time to understand the term "performance correlation".

Consider this analogy: What is the likely correlation between focused studying and getting top grades in class? Usually, studying well tends to translate to higher grades. So, the correlation is said to be high. The reverse may also hold good, as a result of which there tends to be negative correlation between heavy partying and scoring high grades.

Similarly, correlation between asset classes are observed in the investment world.

1. When 'Asset A' performance curve behaves inversely with that of 'Asset B' over time, the correlation is said to be negative, the measure going down to 'minus one'.

2. When 'Asset A' performance curve moves more or less in step with that of 'Asset B' over time, the correlation is said to be positive, the measure going up to 'positive one'.

Consequently, we now have the possibility of using one asset class as a counter to another, to yield a smoother performance curve. The expected outcome is to reduce the volatility of the overall portfolio.

It is extremely important to appreciate that the objective of diversifying across asset classes is primarily to reduce volatility risk, by softening the peaks and troughs, and is generally not intended to increase portfolio value over time.

As a result, the portfolio tends to demonstrates a slightly less volatile performance curve, and the risk of losing capital is mitigated to some extent. The phrase used is "reduced drawdowns" which means reduced capital loss. An important benefit of reduced volatility is reduced stress and increased peace of mind.

To diversify, the three popular asset classes are equity, debt and gold (Exhibit 22).

Exhibit 22: Asset Class Diversification – Common Choices

2-asset Portfolio	3-asset Portfolio
Equity (Capital growth); Debt (Accrual returns)	Equity (Capital growth); Gold (Hedge against inflation and turbulence); Debt (Accrual returns)

The key characteristics of different financial assets are summarized below. Non-physical real estate has been added as a point of comparison (Exhibit 23).

Exhibit 23: Asset Classes Behave Differently

Asset class	Reward	Risk	Volatility
Standard Investments, Basic Asset Diversification			
Equity	Higher potential	Large spikes and drawdowns, periodic crashes	Maximum
Debt	Steady, lower potential	Usually low	Minimal
Further Asset Diversification			
Gold (and other commodities)	Value increases over time, hedge against equity and inflation	Generally low correlation with equity markets, value depends on global trends	Medium
Real Estate (stocks of Real Estate businesses)	Variable	Uncertainty macro and local factors applicable	Variable

Portfolio Diversification Case Study

A vast number of combinations of equity, debt, commodities and real estate assets are available for portfolio construction (for example, refer to Portfoliocharts.com). For the sake of an understanding of the most commonly used asset class combinations, below is data from the US capital markets from Jan 1987 to Oct 2020.

The back tests provide a representative glimpse into the outcome of investing in diverse portfolios comprised of several asset classes, over an extended period of time, in this case over 33 years (Exhibit 24).

Exhibit 24: Back tests For Asset Class Combinations (US Capital Market)

E	US Stock Market = 100%
B	US Bond Market = 50%
EB	US Stock Market = 50% US Bond market = 50%
EBG	US Stock Market = 45% US Bond market = 45% Gold = 10%
Duration	Jan 1987 to Oct 2020 (over 33 years)
Performance indicators	1. Value over time (capital appreciation) 2. Volatility (spikes or 'highs and lows' or drawdowns)

Source: Portfoliovisualizer.com, Oct 2020

The performance and volatility characteristics indicate trends that are commonly observed across asset class combinations. The alarming observation in the value graphs is the massive losses or drawdowns experienced by the pure equity portfolio (Exhibit 25).

Exhibit 25: Back Tests For Asset Class Combinations (Jan 1987 – Oct 2020)

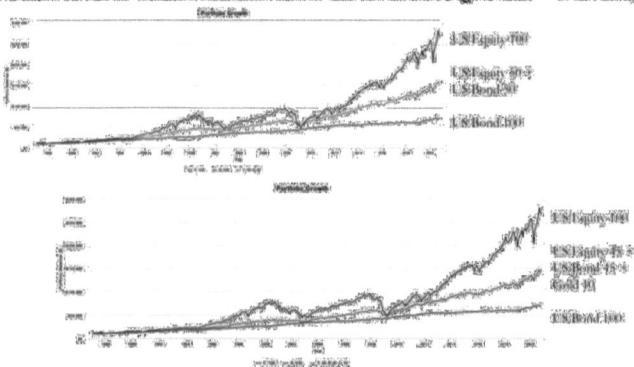

Source: Portfoliovisualizer.com, Oct 2020

To improve understanding, the above two graphs have been represented together in the schematic below (Exhibit 26).

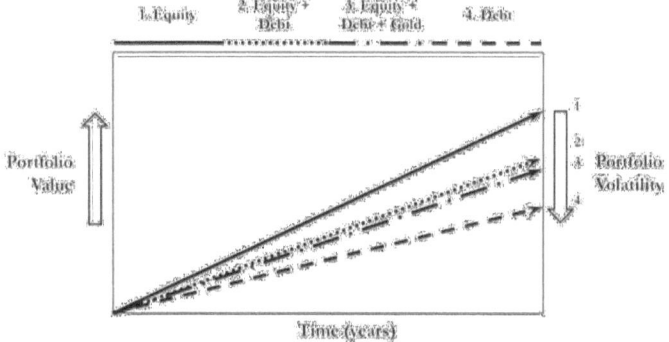

Exhibit 26: Value and Volatility Trends Of Asset Class Combinations

Source: Representation based on data from Portfoliovisualizer.com, Dec 2020

Observation

1. The **portfolio value** of equity turns out to be greater than 'equity + bonds' which is greater than 'equity + bonds + gold', all are greater than pure debt.

2. The **portfolio volatility or drawdown** trends point to equity deeper than 'equity + bonds' which is deeper than 'equity + bonds + gold', all of which are deeper than pure debt.

3. The portfolio value and portfolio volatility trends for 'equity + debt' and 'equity + debt + gold' portfolios typically lie within the envelope formed by the two extreme lines formed by the **'high' of pure equity and the 'low' of pure debt**.

Inference

Overall portfolio performance and volatility characteristics are impacted by the constituent asset classes and the varying correlation levels across assets. Therefore, choosing the appropriate combination of asset classes in the appropriate proportion results in optimal performance and risk, which is a subjective issue, governed by the individual's tolerance to portfolio volatility risk.

For example, applying standard disclaimers, it has been observed that low correlation tends to exist between:

1. Equity and debt assets
2. Equity and gold assets
3. Domestic equity and International equity assets.

Real Estate financial assets, however, do not seem to be as definitive in nature to be able to slot into value and risk characteristics.

Consequently, the following two types of portfolios are often constructed by investors.

Portfolio type 1: Equity + debt assets, often the choice of early stage investors or investors with small to medium portfolios.

Portfolio type 2: Equity (domestic and international) + debt + gold (and/or other commodities), often the choice of experienced investors with medium to large portfolios.

Takeaway (portfolio construction)

The benefit of **portfolio diversification** is to reduce the risk of volatility and capital loss over the long term.

Recommended **steps** to build a portfolio:

Step 1: Combine low-correlation asset classes

Step 2: Globalize the portfolio (add International)

Step 3: Monitor the ratio of the constituent assets

Step 4: Rebalance once or twice a year (recommended).

It's not how much money you make, but how much money you keep, how hard it works for you, and how many generations you keep it for.

– Robert Kiyosaki

Chapter 6

Goal Based Asset Allocation

Question: Having understood the value of portfolio diversification, how would you suggest I actually go about implementing my investment framework – keeping in mind changing goals and priorities of life – over the next 50 years or more?

Answer: We have reached the stage in our discussion where we are in a position to draw out a portfolio diversification strategy and asset allocation roadmap over several decades. Key considerations would be:

1. Assess life goals, financial needs and wants
2. Achieve portfolio growth
3. Reduce portfolio volatility
4. Preserve capital to meet life goals.

A high level project plan of sorts is indicated below, this needs to be implemented by every investor, along with family members, as applicable. This is similar to managing a project.

Financial roadmap assessment (repeat often)

Step 1: Document as-is financial situation (income, expenses, needs, wants, loans, savings, steady state inflow and outflow.

Step 2: Project out your income, savings and expenses over about 5 years, to begin with.

Step 3: Document current financial assets such as bank deposits, mutual funds and so on.

Step 4: For investors in your 20s and 30s, there is no need (or no way!) to quantify retirement needs right away, enough to remember that it would be a future sub-project to understand a drop in income around age 60, assuming retirement age is 60 years, while business income would likely remain for a while longer.

Taking higher risks at younger ages is acceptable, or, even recommended, should you want to beat the bogey of inflation. In general, portfolio risk is reduced with age by reducing equity and increasing debt percentage.

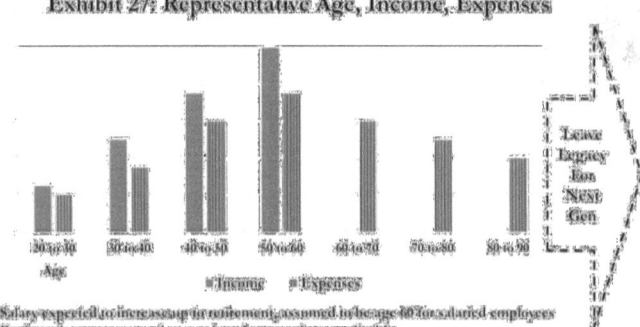

Exhibit 27: Representative Age, Income, Expenses

- Salary expected to increase up to retirement, assumed to be age 60 for salaried employees
- Business income expected to continue longer, where applicable
- Retirement corpus needed to support needs, wants, and healthcare expenses after retirement
- Inflation reduces long term value of retirement corpus
- Some investors may want to leave a legacy for the next generation

For salaried investors without business income, the last several decades of one's life would need to be sustained through returns from the accrued retirement corpus. Investors would need to factor in the negative impacts of inflation (ongoing) and market crashes (uncertain, may happens once every decade or so).

Since expenses after retirement is a subjective situation, three calculations may be kept in mind, to be used as guidelines:

1. How do you grow your portfolio?

The 'Rule of 72' is useful to estimate portfolio returns over the long term:

At 12% interest, money doubles every 6 years.

At 10% interest, money doubles every 7.2 years.

At 9% interest, money doubles every 8 years.

At 6% interest, money doubles every 12 years.

2. How large should your retirement corpus be?

A retirement corpus about 25 to 30 times your annual expenses at retirement may be needed to support you for a period of about 30 years.

3. How much can you consume from your retirement corpus?

As a general guideline, the 'Four Percent Rule' states that you can withdraw 4% of your portfolio each year in retirement for a comfortable life. It was created using historical data on stock and bond returns over a 50-year period. (Source: Investopedia). This is an old formula from the USA, so we to increase the corpus for 5% withdrawal for India, to account for inflation.

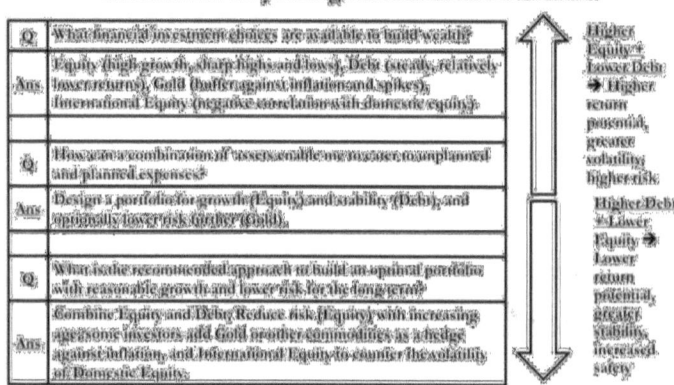

Exhibit 28: Why Design a Diversified Portfolio?

Takeaway (goal based asset allocation)

1. Learning from inferences of the previous sections, asset allocation guidelines suggest a **combination** of equity and debt or a combination of equity, debt and gold (and/or other commodities) invested over the long term, in order to meet life goals.

2. **How much** should you invest? The amount varies from person to person. The answer is **any amount**: start with Rs 1,000 per month or any amount, as early as possible.

The four most dangerous words in investing are: 'this time it's different.

– Sir John Templeton

Asset Allocation Choices for Investors

This section presents a snapshot of investor profiles with varying investing experience, risk tolerance, portfolio diversity and portfolio value.

Investor 1: New to financial roadmap planning, new to mutual funds, attempting to develop a financial roadmap.

Investor 2: Has some experience with mutual funds, ready to plan a financial roadmap and diversify across asset classes.

Investor 3: Fairly experienced with mutual funds and stocks, has developed a long term financial roadmap.

Investor 4: Highly experienced with mutual funds, index funds, ETFs and stocks, has a financial roadmap in place, needs to consolidate stocks, mutual funds, Index funds and ETFs.

The best time to start thinking about your retirement is before the boss does.

– Unknown

Portfolio suggestions

Investor 1 (entry level mutual fund investor): Familiar with conservative, low interest yielding, safe assets such as bank deposits and bank fixed deposits, attempting mutual fund investing for the first time. Or, may have unplanned exposure to mutual funds, based on suggestions from friends, often a result of Recency bias. Needs to develop a phased financial roadmap.

Step 1: Conduct your personal financial audit, including insurance, needs, wants, income and savings, along with up to 5 years projections.

Step 2: Start to build a safe asset bucket with up to 2 years expenses. This may be called Bucket A.

The process of building a bucket for immediate expenses and emergency generally takes a while for young earners, which is quite acceptable. However, the intent must exist, and must be executed. Asset details will be suggested in the next section. We are still at the concept stage.

Step 3: The rest of the investible surplus would need to be invested in Bucket B and Bucket C, in a combination of equity and debt, with a higher allocation towards equity, if possible, commensurate with age and risk tolerance.

Should there be a need to leave a legacy for future generations, a higher allocation to equity would be advised.

Three investor sub profiles have been indicated below, based on ability to tolerate portfolio volatility and associated risk:

1. Aggressive investor profile
2. Moderate investor profile
3. Conservative profile.

The plan is to decrease the quantum of equity assets with increasing age. Further, investors are advised to consider investing in Index for reasons stated above.

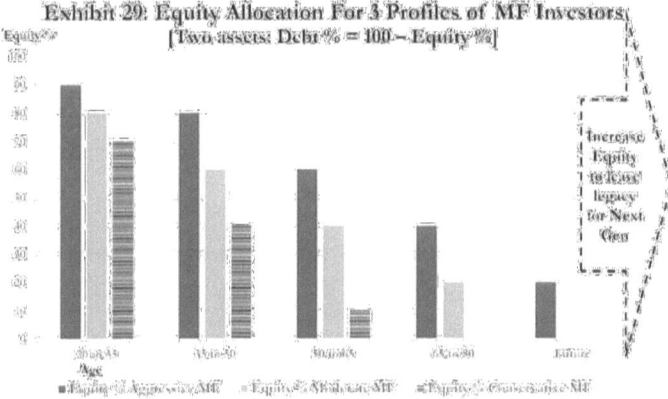

Please refer to Exhibit 34 for a suggested mutual fund portfolio diversification approach.

As always, strongly recommended to transfer from equity to debt as goals approach within the 24 months window.

Why International equities – for experienced investors

From the India investor's perspective, India accounts for only about 3% of the world markets, therefore, vast opportunities exist beyond. Several growth markets exist in the USA, Europe, China, Japan, South Korea and rest of Asia. Market and investment characteristics are often highly diverse. For example, the NASDAQ 100 Index funds or ETFs, though US based, generate an exposure to leading edge high technology businesses with a largely global footprint. Further, the appreciation of the US Dollar versus the Indian Rupee has provided an additional kicker effect in the past.

Why commodities (including gold) – for experienced investors

Commodities such as gold and other metals provide the benefit of hedging when equity markets are uncertain or turbulent, and are also a counter to inflation.

Investor 2 (experienced mutual fund investor): Has some experience with mutual fund investing, not necessarily structured, planning a long term financial roadmap, portfolio size small to medium, ready to diversify into more than two asset classes, seeking to leverage the opportunity of International investing and also take advantage of the cushion of commodities assets.

Step 1: Conduct your personal financial audit, as outlined above, including Insurance, needs, wants, income and savings, along with up to 10 years projections.

Step 2: Start to build a safe asset bucket with up to 2 years expenses. This may be called Bucket A.

The process of building a bucket for immediate expenses and emergency generally takes a while for young earners, which is quite acceptable. However, the intent must exist, and must be executed. Asset details will be suggested in the next section. We are still at the concept stage.

Step 3: The rest of the investible surplus would need to be invested in Bucket B and Bucket C, in a combination of assets with low correlation: equity and debt, with international and gold or other commodities. A higher allocation towards equity is advised, if possible, commensurate with age and risk tolerance.

Should there be a need to leave a legacy for future generations, a higher allocation to equity would be advised.

In order to reduce clutter, the sub profiles such as Aggressive, Moderate and Conservative investor profiles have not been indicated. Suitable assumptions may be made by the reader.

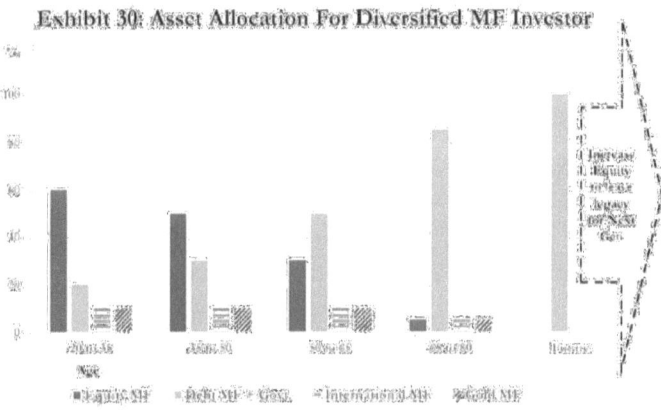

Please refer to Exhibit 34 for a suggested mutual fund portfolio diversification approach.

As always, strongly recommended to transfer from equity to debt as goals approach within the 24 months window.

Investors are advised to consider the Index fund approach. The benefit is reduced clutter, and an easy to manage portfolio.

Investor 3 (mutual fund and stocks investor): Fairly experienced with indirect equity (mutual funds) and Index funds across several asset classes, has a long term roadmap, portfolio size medium to large, ready to diversify into direct equity (stocks), seeking to consolidate the portfolio.

Step 1: Conduct your personal financial audit, as outlined above, including Insurance, needs, wants, income and savings, along with up to 10 years projections.

Step 2: Start to build a safe asset bucket with up to 2 years expenses. This may be called Bucket A.

The process of building a bucket for immediate expenses and emergency generally takes a while for young earners, which is quite acceptable. However, the intent must exist, and must be executed. Asset details will be suggested in the next section. We are still at the concept stage.

Step 3: The rest of the investible surplus would need to be invested in Bucket B and Bucket C, in a combination of assets with low correlation: direct and indirect equity and debt, with international and gold or other commodities. A higher allocation towards equity is advised, if possible, commensurate with age and risk tolerance. The overall plan is to diversify through equity, debt, international equity, commodities and direct equities, leverage the value of Index funds and optionally to allocate some Fun money for learning purposes. The Fun component may be used for investing into sectoral mutual funds and direct equities that appear interesting enough to risk a small percentage of the portfolio in order to earn higher than usual reward, with informed risk.

Should there be a need to leave a legacy for future generations, a higher allocation to equity would be advised.

Investors with a long roadmap are advised to consider the Index fund approach, and reduce clutter early in life.

In order to reduce clutter, the sub profiles such as Aggressive, Moderate and Conservative investor profiles have not been indicated. Suitable assumptions may be made by the reader.

Please refer to Exhibit 34 for a suggested mutual fund portfolio diversification approach.

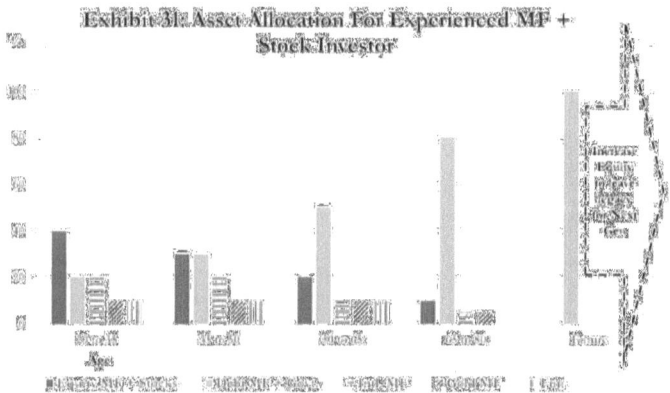

Please refer to Exhibit 12 for suggested stock picking approach.

As always, strongly recommended to transfer from equity to debt as goals approach within the 24 months window.

Investors are advised to consider the Index fund approach. The benefit is reduced clutter, and an easy to manage portfolio.

Investor 4 (experienced mutual fund, ETF and stocks investor): Highly experienced with indirect equity (mutual fund) and direct equity (stock) assets, has a long term roadmap, invested across several asset classes, portfolio size medium to large, consisting of a combination of active mutual funds, index investing and ETF, looking to further leverage the Demat platform and lower fees for Exchange Traded Funds (ETF). Younger investors with a long roadmap may also consider this approach, and reduce clutter early in life.

Step 1: Conduct your personal financial audit, as outlined above, including Insurance, needs, wants, income and savings, along with 10 years or higher projections.

Step 2: Start to build a safe asset bucket with up to 2 years expenses. This may be called Bucket A.

Asset details will be suggested in the next section. We are still at the concept stage.

Step 3: The rest of the investible surplus would need to be invested in Bucket B and Bucket C, in a combination of assets with low correlation: direct and indirect equity and debt, with international and gold or other commodities. A higher allocation towards equity is advised, if possible, commensurate with age and risk tolerance.

The overall plan is to diversify through equity, debt, international equity, commodities and direct equities, leverage the value of Index funds and ETFs, and optionally provision of a small allocation of Fun money for learning purposes. The Fun component may be used for investing into sectoral mutual funds and direct equities that appear interesting enough to risk a small percentage of the portfolio in order to earn higher than usual reward, with informed risk.

Should there be a need to leave a legacy for future generations, a higher allocation to equity would be advised.

Investors with a long roadmap are advised to consider the Index fund approach, and reduce clutter early in life.

In order to reduce clutter, the sub profiles such as Aggressive, Moderate and Conservative investor profiles have not been indicated. Suitable assumptions may be made by the reader.

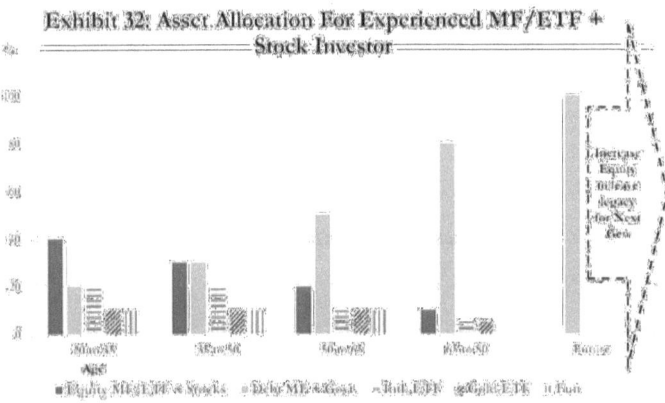

Please refer to Exhibit 34 for suggested mutual fund portfolio diversification approach.

Please refer to Exhibit 12 for suggested stock picking approach.

As always, strongly recommended to transfer from equity to debt as goals approach within the 24 months window.

Takeaway (asset allocation)

1. Long term financial security requires diligent planning, saving and investing, with some risk tolerance.

2. Beating inflation is a critical requirement.

3. Invest in **diversified** asset with low performance correlation between them.

4. Most investors reduce **risk** with age by increasing the amount of lower risk, steady yield assets.

5. Should there be a need to leave a legacy for future generations, a higher allocation to **equity** would be advised.

You should have a strategic asset allocation mix that assumes that you don't know what the future is going to hold.

– Ray Dalio

Chapter 7
Asset Reallocation

Question: The pieces of the puzzle seem to be falling into place in my mind. However, I need to understand an important concept: how are the pieces adjusted over time in order to meet changing priorities of needs, wants and capital preservation, not to forget emergencies and pandemics, in the midst of growth and drawdowns?

Answer: First, a disclaimer. The portfolio framework and approach we have discussed is generic in nature. Individual implementations would vary based on assets, liabilities, family situation, targets during various stages of the life journey and ability to tolerate volatility and risk.

A multi-bucket approach works well, with each bucket serving a different timeframe, comprising of appropriate financial assets, with their own unique performance, volatility and risk characteristics.

Exhibit 33: Long Term Three Bucket Portfolio Concept

	Bucket A	Set aside 2 to 3 years emergency funds, needs and wants expenses in easily accessible Bank deposits and relatively low volatile Debt mutual funds.
	\multicolumn{2}{l|}{Apply portfolio diversification guidelines (80:20 or 70:30 or 60:30:10 or other) to the remainder of your portfolio, split across buckets B and C.}
	Bucket B	Allocate future expenses (beyond 3, to 10, 20, 30, 40, 50, 60, 70... years] to higher risk, higher reward Equity assets, optionally hedged with Gold (or other Commodities), for expenses and retirement.
	Bucket C	Safe, Government backed assets for part of retirement corpus.

Steps:

1. Define personal financial roadmap and buckets.

2. Build '**Bucket A**' as soon as possible, for emergency and ongoing use. Young earners will take time to fill the insurance and near term bucket. Start with Rs 1,000 per month or any amount possible. Don't give up!

3. Subsequently, start building '**Bucket B**' for the long term and '**Bucket C**' for retirement (about 50% allocation each).

4. Reallocate based on market events or based on need.

5. Transfer to 'Bucket A' about 2 to 3 years before any expected major goal is due to be reached.

When implemented right, this portfolio structure contains clearly defined buckets for specific time durations. The objective is to maintain a clean and manageable portfolio. While bank deposit and similar types of instruments are familiar to many, they are just not adequate to beat inflation and to support long term financial success. Equity exposure enables one to meet long term goals and provision for retirement.

Investors with limited experience and with small to medium size portfolios are advised to keep the portfolio simple (Exhibit 34). For those not aware, the Indian Nifty 50 Index contains the top 50 businesses by market cap (similar to the S&P 500 Index which is the top 500 companies by market cap in the USA).

Exhibit 34: Long Term Three Bucket Portfolio Implementation [For small to medium portfolio, entry level investor]

Bucket A	Scientific 3m day as emergency funds and expenses in easily accessible Bank deposits and regular/low volatile Debt Mutual funds.	• Savings bank accounts • Auto sweep Bank deposits • Short Term Debt Mutual fund.	Use A for ongoing spends. Rebalance / transfer from 'B' to 'A'.
	Apply proportionate reinvestment gains (20% of D) during periodic rebalance of your set of portfolios across buckets B and C.		
Bucket B	All near future expenses (3 to 10, 20, 40, 50, 60, 70+ years). Higher risk, higher reward Equity assets hedged with Gold.	• Nifty Index fund • Gold MF / Gov Gold Bond.	Spot based earmarked asset based reallocation between PF, B and C.
Bucket C	Safe Government backed assets for years of retirement corpus.	• PPF, NPS • EPF, VRF (Salaried investor)	

Investors with greater experience or with medium to large portfolios often diversify by means of global exposure, and they also temper volatility by hedging with commodities such as gold and/or other metals.

Some experienced investors add one actively managed Hybrid Equity Fund to introduce a small debt component in the long term 'Bucket B'. This approach, however, needs careful monitoring, since actively managed funds tend to play musical chairs and go up and down the returns charts.

Such profile of investors often manage diverse portfolios. However, the opportunity to simplify and streamline portfolio seems to exist for most investors (Exhibit 35).

Exhibit 35: Long Term Three Bucket Portfolio Implementation (For medium to large portfolio, experienced investor)

Bucket A	Scalable 2 to 4 years emergency funds and expenses in easily accessible Bank deposits and relatively low volatile Debt mutual funds.	• Savings bank accounts • Auto-sweep Bank deposits • Short Term Debt Mutual Fund	Use 'A' for ongoing spends.
	Apply goal planning across annuity incomes (20-30 years) and other means to consider equity to call portfolio split across Buckets B and C.		Periodic transfer from 'B' to 'A'.
Bucket B	Allocate for year's spends 10 to 20, 30, 40, 50, 60, 70+ years or higher risk, higher reward Equity assets, mingled with Gold and other Commodities.	• Stocks • Nifty 50 Index Fund / ETF • International Equity MF / ETF • Commodities MF / ETF (Gov, Gold) Bonds	Need based transfer to rebalance reallocation between 'A', 'B' and 'C'.
Bucket C	Safe, Government backed assets for purpose of retirement corpus.	• PPF or NPS • EPF / APF (salaried investors)	

Takeaway (3-bucket portfolio)

1. Consider the simple, long term, **3-bucket, goal based, asset approach**.

2. First **provision** funds in 'Bucket A', then 'Bucket B' and 'Bucket C' on an ongoing basis.

3. Maintain approximate asset allocation **ratios** as per plan.

4. Transfer **equity to debt** as goals approach (24 to 36 months is relatively safe).

5. **Reallocate** in order to maintain ratios, in the event of a major market event or an upcoming planned expense.

Wealth is the ability to fully experience life.

– Henry David Thoreau

Chapter 8
Personal Income Tax Benefits

Parent to child: One of the incentives of investing in capital markets is the government provision to save personal Income Tax. From the Indian investors' perspective, the following table may help as a ready reckoner. Detailed discussions on personal Income Tax planning are beyond the scope of this discussion. Exhibit 36 lists core tax saving options.

Exhibit 36: Tax Planning Options for Indian Investors (1)

#	Tax Saving Instruments	Priority	Remarks
1	Life Insurance Premium	Top priority, mandatory	Choose Term Insurance not "endowment" or money-back plans
2	Health Insurance Premium	Top priority, mandatory	Consider add-on (e.g. Illness) options, since initial coverage may become inadequate over time
3	Public Provident Fund (PPF)	Top priority, strongly recommended for salaried and non-salaried	Safe, tax-free withdrawal, no annuity compulsion, cannot be attached by creditors
4	National Pension Scheme (NPS)	High priority, recommended for salaried and non-salaried	Safe, equity and debt options, complex tax at withdrawal, partially tax-free, partially compulsory for taxable annuity

Further tax saving options may be considered, as applicable (Exhibit 37).

Exhibit 37: Tax Planning Options for Indian Investors (2)

#	Tax Saving Instruments	Priority	Remarks
1	Employee Provident Fund (EPF)	Top priority, mandatory for salaried employees	Fully tax-free withdrawal on retirement
2	Voluntary Provident Fund (VPF)	High priority, optional for salaried employees, recommended	Fully tax-free withdrawal on retirement
3	Equity Linked Savings Scheme (ELSS)	May be used mainly to build Equity component	Subject to market linked volatility and risk, lock-in period applies
4	Sovereign Gold Bonds	Recommended, may be considered	Track international gold price, small interest paid, tax-free on maturity
5	Tax Saving Bank Fixed Deposits	Low priority	Interest rate decided by bank, lock-in period applies

Takeaway (tax benefits)

1. Term life **insurance** and health insurance are top priority; in addition, consider accident insurance.

2. Absolutely **avoid** "endowment" and "money back" type of life insurance; only choose simple Term insurance policies.

3. Consider augmenting **health** insurance with suitable "top-up" plans as the years go by.

4. NPS and PPF are preferred options to build the long term retirement **debt** corpus.

5. While EPF is mandatory, VPF is recommended for **salaried** employees.

6. ELSS may be used **initially** to build the equity component in the portfolio and simultaneously save tax.

The taxpayer: that's someone who works for the federal government, but doesn't have to take a civil service examination.

– Ronald Reagan

Chapter 9
Conclusion

Parent to Child: We began our discussion with the backdrop of 2020 being widely regarded among the most forgettable years in living memory. Individuals, families, communities, industries and countries have been impacted in multiple dimensions, from personal to inter-personal to careers to industry to economy and lives lost.

There is no certainty that another lethal virus is not going to sweep us over once again in the near future. The workforce must be prepared to face employment risks. Owners of businesses must be prepared to face business and organizational risks. Further, market returns are neither predictable nor have they indicated upward trends over the past few decades.

Age and goal based investment planning across diverse asset classes is the only way out to achieve life goals for individuals and their families in a systematic manner.

With increasing age, the portfolio may need to be tweaked, depending on investing experience, ability to tolerate risk, and the retirement corpus that would need to be consumed or maintained.

The table below indicates investment assets that may be considered by young earners, as they begin their careers and progress towards middle age (Exhibit 38).

Exhibit 38: Long Term Investment Roadmap To Consider (1) *

Age range	Short Term Debt	Debt, Gold (Govt)	Equity	Equity Linked Savings Scheme	International Equities	Gold or other Commodities
20 to 35	Bank, Short Term Debt MF	PPF or SPS, EPF, VPF, Gold bonds	Nifty Index MF + Stocks	Build Equity component and reduce tax	Recommended	Recommended
35 to 50	Bank, Short Term Debt MF	PPF or SPS, EPF, VPF, Gold bonds	Nifty Index MF + Stocks	May not need	Recommended	Recommended

* Keep house as separate fixed investment

As retirement age approaches for salaried employees, or when business income is likely to reduce, investment options may be adjusted (Exhibit 39).

Exhibit 39: Long Term Investment Roadmap To Consider (2) *

Age range	Short Term Debt	Debt, Gold (Govt)	Equity	Equity Linked Savings Scheme	International Equities	Gold or other Commodities
50 to 65	Bank, Short Term Debt MF	PPF or SPS, EPF, APF, Gold bonds	Nifty Index MF + Stocks	May not need	Recommended	Recommended
65 to 80	Bank, Short Term Debt MF	PPF or SPS, Gold bonds	Depends on portfolio size and risk appetite	May not need	Depends on portfolio size and risk appetite	Depends on portfolio size and risk appetite
80+	Bank, Short Term Debt MF	PPF or NPS, Gold bonds	Depends on portfolio size and risk appetite	May not need	Depends on portfolio size and risk appetite	Depends on portfolio size and risk appetite

* Keep house as separate fixed investment

Since expenses after retirement is a subjective situation, three calculations may be kept in mind, to be used as guidelines:

1. **How do you grow your portfolio?**

   The 'Rule of 72' is useful to estimate portfolio returns over the long term:

   At 12% interest, money doubles every 6 years.

   At 10% interest, money doubles every 7.2 years.

   At 9% interest, money doubles every 8 years.

   At 6% interest, money doubles every 12 years.

2. **How large should your retirement corpus be?**

   A retirement corpus about 25 to 30 times your annual expenses at retirement may be needed to support you for a period of about 30 years.

3. **How much can you consume from your retirement corpus?**

   As a general guideline, the 'Four Percent Rule' states that you can withdraw 4% of your portfolio each year in retirement for a comfortable life. It was created using historical data on stock and bond returns over a 50-year period. (Source: Investopedia). This is an old formula from the USA, so we to increase the corpus for 5% withdrawal for India, to account for inflation.

Takeaway

You are responsible for your life and your life goals:

1. Own your life goals and build your financial roadmap.
2. Be wary of advisors, agents and brokers should they try to mis-sell products and services.
3. Outsource with care.

Mindset

1. Develop a long term, calm mindset towards saving and investing.
2. Plan your investment journey.
3. Start by regularly investing any amount, as early as possible.

Career skills

1. Relevant skills will drive you towards a career of value.
2. Continuously sharpen existing and emerging skills.
3. Develop secondary skills not in conflict with your employment, such as teaching, blogging, writing, and so on.
4. Secondary skills would come in handy after retirement, being mental and financial cushions.

Plan and manage your portfolio

1. Assess your income, needs, wants, savings and investments regularly.

2. Diversify, simplify, and invest long term – you only need Bucket A, Bucket B, Bucket C – **this is my learning**.

3. Invest regularly - automated or tactical - but not blindly.

4. Transfer funds to Bucket A as goals approach.

5. Do not panic in the event of a market crash.

6. Your 'Bucket A' will see you through while the market recovers in due course.

Stay invested at the right time

1. Extreme market volatility and spikes (crashes and pullbacks) are observed almost every decade.

2. It is well understood that stock markets tend to gains over short, concentrated bursts.

3. It is critical to leverage the sudden and sharp upward movements when maximum gains take place, by reallocating funds from debt to equity.

Nomination, Documentation, Will

1. Ensure Joint holding or Nomination, as appropriate.

2. Document physical and financial assets.

3. Document insurance claim processes and contacts.

4. Write a will when you own financial and physical assets.

This document is an attempt to compress observations, research and lessons learnt into a few pages. There would be obvious limitations in terms of completeness of explanations.

Please use this document as a template for reference. Do keep it alive. As you learn, collaborate and walk down the path of informed financial success. Spread the word. Discuss with unbiased advisors. Secure your Life and Health. Stay away from sales persons selling dubious products and services. Learn from mistakes, don't worry too much, and always have a lot of fun!

With best wishes to you and your family for a lifetime of happy investing and continued career success!

To make money in stocks, you need to have vision to see them, courage to buy them and patience to hold them. Patience is the rarest of the three.

– Thomas Phelps

Acknowledgements

This book embodies lessons learnt over several decades. Initially, as a child, observing and listening to my Dad as he went about investing in stocks well before the internet and digitization of financial assets. Besides books, I have learnt from print and TV media such as Bloomberg, CNBC and Economic Times and several valuable online resources, primarily, Freefincal, Marcellus, Moneycontrol, Morningstar, Screener, Value Research Online and Yahoo Finance.